HUMAN NATURE

EX LIBRIS

HUMAN NATURE

THE JAPANESE GARDEN
OF
PORTLAND, OREGON

BRUCE TAYLOR HAMILTON

JAPANESE GARDEN SOCIETY

OF OREGON

(front cover)
Japanese Garden's traditional Tea House
from the upper pond area of the Strolling Pond Garden.
(Ron Cronin Photograph)

(back cover)
Autumn-red Acer palmatum maple leaves.
(Allan Mandell Photograph)

(facing title page)
June brings iris blossoms to Portland's Japanese Garden. These plants (Iris ensata or Iris kaempferi) surround the Zigzag Bridge in the Strolling Pond Garden. An azalea (Rhododenron indicum) stands behind the the lower pond's snow-viewing lantern.
(Ron Cronin photograph)

Production of this work was supported in part by a generous in-kind donation by Wy'east Color, Inc. of Portland.

Second Printing, revised.

Library of Congress Cataloging-in-Publication Data

Hamilton, Bruce Taylor, 1940 -

The Japanese Garden of Portland, Oregon.

p.   cm.

ISBN 0-9645514-0-3

CIP

Printed in Singapore.

5 4 3 2

FOR

WILLIAM DALLAS WON

WHO QUIETLY ENCOURAGED ME TO WRITE

Maple trunks near the Entry Gate inside the Garden. It is one of several trees brought to the site from the University of Oregon Dental School in the early 1990s.

(Bruce Lellman photograph)

CONTENTS

A Japanese garden is not only a place for the cultivation of trees and flowering shrubs, but one that provides secluded leisure, rest, repose, meditation and sentimental pleasure . . . . The Garden speaks to all the senses not just to the mind alone.

Professor Takuma Tono
Designer of Portland's Japanese Garden

Professor Takuma Tono,
designer of Portland's
Japanese Garden
(Japanese Garden Archive)

As with numerous places in Portland's Japanese Garden, the steps between the lower and upper paths of the Natural Garden entice the visitor from one beautiful spot to another. Along with so many of the plants and materials in the Garden, these stones were recycled—from the old Civic Auditorium.

(Rick Schafer—American Landscapes—photograph)

A PAUSE AT THE GATE:
AN INTRODUCTION

I t is tucked into a cusp, a bend, in Portland's West Hills, situated at about five hundred feet above sea level on an ancient landslide that has undergone relatively slow, though continuous, movement for over one century. Portland, Oregon's internationally recognized Japanese Garden beckons visitors from home and abroad to enter its unique confines.

Today, (except to those who have the eye to discern otherwise) it seems mature; it strikes one that this has been here a long time. Yet, this remarkable place is not simply young, it is still in its infancy. Little more than thirty years old, it represents a melding of Japanese traditional garden forms with American hurry.

When measured against its inspirational precursors in Japan, many of which are hundreds of years old, the Portland garden has come to a "maturity" with blinding swiftness. It stands as a testament to a number of positive and honorable human attributes—the best of human nature. What the visitor sees today is the result of the efforts by hundreds of dedicated persons who have given years of time and care and foresight to match the vision that a group of Portland civic and political leaders had as the 1950s turned into the 1960s.

The story of the Japanese Garden is their story, persons both named and anonymous. It is a tale of heart and soul, that reflects

Surrounded by cedar, maple, pieris and rhododendron plants is this stone from the Ripple Brook area of the Clackamas River.

(Allan Bruce Zee photograph)

*Bridges in a garden often are symbolic,
as is the Stone Bridge
at the western edge of the Flat Garden.
It was one of the first elements
of the Garden,
placed here in November 1963
under the on-site supervision
of the Garden's designer,
Professor Takuma Tono.*

(Allan Mandell photograph)

both the wonder that is a Japanese garden and the human touch that is such an elemental part of what these gardens bestow. Each person who visits the Garden might pause to reflect on its transcendent beauty while noting in all its corners and swales the soulful and altruistic contributions made by single persons, garden groups, nursery people, gardeners (both civic and private), corporations, kindred folks, business and political leaders in both the United States and Japan, volunteers, staff, hard-working Board members, and the City of Portland itself.

The story of the Japanese Garden Society of Oregon is one of tradition, dedication, commitment, of success. The story is, surprisingly, about a word that was not in vogue when the first planning took place, but is central to much that is in the spirit of Portland, of Oregon as a whole, and increasingly deep in the consciousness of Americans in general. It is a story of recycling.

A grand and gradual recycling of special plantings and of other materials is one of the strengths of this Garden. Donations of hundreds of plants now seen in the Garden have come from numerous sources, including local nurseries (especially members of the Oregon Nurserymen's Association whose plant-matter gifts fill the Garden), garden clubs, private citizens, and from construction sites where new freeways, parking garages, or other new structures could have meant the destruction of some of the more important Japanese cut-leaf maples and pines that are now integral to the design balance of the Garden. There are over twenty thread-leaf maples in the Garden that came from Sellwood Park, as did the camellias that form the Camellia Tunnel entrance to the Strolling Pond Garden. Many of the Garden's ilex and pieris had been used at the 1959 Oregon Centennial site in north Portland.

In almost all of the five areas that make up this garden are rec-

HUMAN NATURE

tangular granite stepping stones and bridges and entry paths. Anticipating the reconstruction of the city's venerable Civic Auditorium, the Board made its bid for recycling the granite entry steps, which were removed when the auditorium was refurbished.

A Japanese garden can be "read" for it is full of symbolism and short-hand representations of nature. Unlike western gardens, whose aspects are rarely symbolic, everything in a Japanese garden is open to interpretation. Small trees represent large, stones represent fish or ships, turtles or cranes. Gatherings of stones can represent trees, can be male or female or priests, among other things. The internationally famous designer of Japanese Gardens, Tokyo Professor Takuma Tono (who so carefully laid out the Portland Garden's grand design in the 1960s) felt that the "fundamental aim of landscape gardening in Japan rests upon 'viewing, instructing and consoling'. . . Gardens are intended to break the connection with the outside world, . . . and to produce a fresh sensation conducive to full enjoyment of aestheticism of Nature."

 The Japanese garden is for the visitor to enjoy, to take in. It is not a place were one needs botanical knowledge. In fact, the case could be made that trying to learn the names of the plants may be contrary to what a Japanese garden is all about. More important than memorizing the Latin name for the black pine is to understand that in Japan this tree represents the masculine, courage; in the same manner the red pine represents the feminine and delicacy.

 There are a number of concepts at work in a Japanese garden. Much is made of "borrowed scenery" or "borrowed view"(*shakkei*), with the prime example in the Portland Garden being the remarkable vista across the city toward the Cascades and Mount Hood. But varied views are also made available as the seasons change by the careful

*Bridges in a garden can be real.
Portland's Japanese Garden
has numerous bridges.
They are used by visitors
as they walk through its environs.
They are constructed of stone,
earth and wood.
The best known is the Moon Bridge
in the Strolling Pond Garden.*

(David Whetstone photograph)

*Tricks of scale, real or implied, are part
of experiencing a Japanese garden.
The scale can be grand,
as in the Western redcedar grove's
massive native dark boles.
Underneath is a carpet of mosses,
the smallest plants in the Garden.*

(William Robinson photograph)

opening of the shoji screens in Garden buildings, such as the Portland Garden's Pavilion. Tono felt strongly about borrowed scenery. He wrote:

> The use of a small piece of ground is characteristic of the Japanese garden. Although the garden itself is not so large, if the scenery behind is fortunately enough of a beautiful forest or a mountain, we utilize this outside scenery as a part of the particular garden structure, presenting an expansive appearance including those background features.

Another, and often forgotten, concept is that of "captured alive" (*ikedori*), which is a critical element in the Garden's success. Look at the fortunate enclosing backdrop of hillside forest as well as the "captured" Douglas firs and Western red cedars, both of which frame and center this Garden. The trunks of these large conifers have been made to frame a number of views throughout the Garden, providing *shakkei*.

There are tricks of scale in a Japanese garden. Western gardens are often small vistas that move to large ones—that carry the eye from the immediate to the distant. Japanese gardens work from big to small—often drawing the eye to the smallest assemblage, one that mimics and parallels larger and longer views.

The concept of "hide and reveal" (*miegakura*) is as subtle as it sounds. Plantings, the placement of stones, the route of pathways, all give the Garden wanderer constantly changing views—a kind of "now you see it, now you don't" that brings to the eye, and hence all the other senses, a slowly evolving kaleidoscope.

The visitor to the Garden soon becomes aware that every step brings a new view, a vista or an intimacy that slightly syncopates as the viewer moves from one spot to the next. Yet, there is flow and

HUMAN NATURE

development and ebb. Long views briefly are exposed, only to be curtained off by something close, only to be revealed again as the eyes, and the other senses, let themselves be taken over.

The visitor is not meant to gasp and be in awe of the Garden, the visitor instead is made reflective. The Garden is meant to calm, to soothe and, as one photographer noted, it is "to fill you or to empty you." Any place and every place in the Garden is construed to be a view, a glimpse or a vista—often called *hapo nirami*, the "all around view."

It is hard to overstate the importance of water to Japanese gardens. Tono believed that "water is certainly an almost indispensable feature of the Japanese gardens." Water in repose, as in the various ponds, brings peace and a stillness to the heart. But the sound of running water is especially significant. Standing next to running water has a Zen quality that all who fly fish understand. Professor Tono suggested that "water receives its highest regard when it moves or makes a sound. . . . As a lake, river, stream, torrent or cascade, ornamental water may be seen. . . . It is essential that a garden should be cool and refreshing in summer which is the period when Japanese enjoy a garden the most." Even where there is no water—as in a sand and stone garden—the implication of water lies at the heart of the Japanese garden.

Stone has a unique place in the Japanese garden, one that is essential to its gardening traditions. "It is no exaggeration to say that the success or failure of a garden entirely depends upon the stone composition," wrote Professor Tono. "We treat natural stones as materials which have vital factors. That is because we feel life and soul in the natural stones which are frequently used as an idealistic and also as a realistic representation." Tono felt that "stones in some cases constitute the skeleton of the garden."

*The garden experience
can bring the visitor
into the details
of plants, stones and structures.
Here are spring-time blossoms
gracing a pieris plant
in the Garden.*

(Jerry Stelmack photograph)

Garden designers use a variety of materials to focus the eye of the viewer. Fences can be employed as backdrop or enclosure for plantings, as here in the Flat Garden.

(Bruce Lellman photograph)

Throughout Japanese gardens stones are used for various purposes. While they are often chosen for their own elegant lines and bulk, stones also are used to represent tortoises or cranes, fish or ships at sea. They affect the viewer's sense of scale and they are used to mimic nature, often in a reduced size. Stones placed in a garden should have the look that natural forces were in charge of the final resting place of each, not the intervening human hand. In some gardens, the largest stone is called the "guardian stone." Sometimes a long curving boulder can be called a "recumbent ox" stone. In fact, most large stones lying on their sides are referred to as "reclining stones," those upright called "standing stones." There can be angling stones and sentinel stones, worshipping stones and garden-viewing stones, among hundreds of others that have specific functions and placements in Japanese gardens. Professor Tono is remembered as saying: "It's a stone in its natural state, but when it's broken it becomes a rock, as in crushed rock."

But natural stones are not the only stone features. Placed at carefully chosen locations, carved stone lanterns dot gardens. If one were to walk Portland's Garden only to find the lanterns, it would be immediately clear that these are absolutely on target in their placement. Situated at junctions of trails, or to light some of the water basins or well locations, or placed to lend drama or balance to a view, these lanterns snap into sight as one of the many surprises that are part of what a Japanese garden brings to the open-eyed and open-minded visitor—all part of hide and reveal. They often will come into sight slowly, as if one notices a good friend has been standing nearby, unnoticed.

Professor Tono felt that lanterns "do much to humanize the landscape." At another time he wrote: "Among the garden ornaments, probably there is nothing so impressive as the stone lantern which first attracts the eye of a visitor to a Japanese garden." Natural stones form the "skeleton" of a garden, a structure that is added to by sand and smaller stones, structures, lanterns and pathways.

The full embodiment of a garden comes from the plants. No matter how spare a garden is its rendering is made complete with things growing, be they only moss. Their changing features are like the clothing of the garden, the seasonal garments.

The plantings in a Japanese garden, so different from the Western gardening tradition, are used for a balance that comes from how they work together or contrast with each other. A garden is completed with the plants, evergreen and deciduous trees and shrubs, the mosses and bamboo. Tono felt strongly that "the skeleton of a planting design consists of evergreens as the fundamental material. Deciduous trees are used to accentuate the planting value and function of each group."

The visitor will observe that plantings of similar trees (for example black pines) are rarely in even numbers; groupings of three and five are much more attuned to the Japanese sense of proportion. The shapes of plants—their forms—often are due to the deft pruning gardeners have used over time to work out symmetry or asymmetry when either is desired. The evergreen is balanced with the deciduous, the various flowering plants are laid out to be featured when their glory time comes. In spring and fall, the daily changes are as feverish as a Japanese garden will get. No dazzle of acres of roses, or tulips or sunflowers, just the subtle, subdued panoply made more delicious by what variety, timing, balancing and patience can bring.

Throughout the Garden there are supports attached to certain plants. These are artfully done, as with so many things Japanese, and are meant to be seen-—added design elements in the Garden. The horizontal bamboo poles (*soedake*) are designed to straighten ever-

*There are times when plants are
backdrop for built shapes,
as with this low bamboo fence
tucked beneath the green leaves
of the Garden's one weeping cherry.*

(Allan Mandell photograph)

In a the Flat Garden,
raked Shirakawa sand
performs its leveling sea-like role
in contrast to relief of earth and stone,
and the ever-changing
backdrop of shrubs and trees.

(Allan Mandell photograph)

green branches that tend to turn upward, or (in cold climates) to protect plants with strong horizontal branches from breaking under the weight of winter snows. Other trees can be seen with triangular supports (*kazayokeshichu*), which stabilize a newly planted tree at the point where the supports are tied onto the trunk or branch. Once a tree is fully rooted, the support is removed.

Be aware of the use of paths and how they move you from one special place to another. They are not haphazard routes through a wilderness, but integrated elements of a garden. They are at turns broad and stepped, or winding, or paved, or gravel, each with its own purpose, its own integration. "Garden walks are laid mainly for the purpose of affording walking pleasure," wrote Tono. They lead you. They carry you back. They help you know when to stop. They often change your pace.

Part of these paths are the bridges that bring the walker to the water. Some are flat, or arched, some inviting one to stop, others with great vistas of a garden. Some bridges make the visitor part of the scene.

Finally, a word about the gardeners. Yes, much of what they do is maintenance, caring for the overwhelming demands of thousands of plants. Even with this seemingly routine activity, each gardener has to have an eye for each plant's past and its future, and how it fits in its own assemblage. There used to be an adage that when you received a good haircut, no one could tell you had a haircut. It holds true that the gardeners must do the same with the plants under their care.

In many ways a gardener in a Japanese garden is like the grafting surgeon. A kind of "grafting" is done every day, all year, year in and year out, as plants are pruned and staked, added, deleted or moved, as stones and lanterns and compatible structures are integrated into

HUMAN NATURE

the whole. As with the surgeon's graft, the operation is a success if the viewer does not notice the addition to or deletion from the whole, if the gardener continues to make the garden appear seamless and complete.

A former landscape director or the Portland Garden, Masayuki Mizuno, states: "This Garden has progressed much faster than gardens in my homeland. It might have taken fifty years in Japan to do what was done here in five." He adds that one should not view this as "impatience" but as a "challenge" to the gardener.

Mizuno suggests caring for the Garden can be as simple as taking a "look at the ground conditions—and you see everything—the spirit of the ground." He pauses and amplifies: "The essence of the garden is the spirit of the earth." Gardening is simply, he concludes, "taking care of the earth."

In fact, the gardeners have little time to take on major changes. The awesome number of "demanding" plants keep them transplanting, shaping, mowing, raking, blowing, removing needles and leaves, adding and retying supports, feeding and spraying (for insects and fungus), dividing bulbs, tending moss, moving stones, snapping off pine candles, and a thousand other tasks to simply maintain a garden. It is all the balance between the understated human touch and the unrestrained power of nature. The balance is truly "human nature."

Arising out of the tradition of family gardens—first developed in China and brought to Japan—Japanese gardens were considered "protectors" of a family. Transferred to the more public gardens was the concept that they brought peace and good health and even prosperity to those who visited and learned from them. Visitors to these

Raked sand is matched with stones in the severe Zen gardens. In Portland's exemplar, Shirakawa sand from Japan contrasts with lovely stones from Oregon's Cascade Range.

(Allan Mandell photograph)

The Garden's normal color is green. Evergreens and mosses maintain this hue. After leaves bud and before the vibrant colors of autumn, it is green that is the common summer color of other plants. That is the subtle palette, the backdrop to winter's snow, spring's blossoming, and the wild show of fall.

(Ron Cronin photograph)

gardens have the feeling that each garden has a personality of its own—almost human—that influences those who come into contact with it. It is much the same as meeting a calm and sage person during the course of one's day—and being positively influenced by that contact.

"A garden is a medium to give people a moment to lift them up, giving themselves something they did not have before," noted former Portland landscape director Hoichi Kurisu. He added, "It is uplifting—a moment to feel a revolution. It is to inspire." While a Japanese garden is contemplative, it can inspire a person to action outside its confines in the day-to-day world.

The Japanese garden has been termed a "reticent" version of nature, one that is "symbolic." Never an exact copy, the Japanese garden is an ennobling idealization. It is designed to appear as nature in its pristine state—a reduced version. This is done by the human mind and the human kind. The Japanese garden is after all a wonderful example of artifice, of the ability of human beings to manipulate nature, and to take that artifice on as intensely real. The Japanese garden is the highest of human endeavor. The human, the visitor, completes the garden. The Japanese garden is human nature.

Portland's Japanese Garden takes full advantage of its remarkable site.
With a backdrop of Washington Park, the layout by acclaimed Japanese garden designer
Takuma Tono melds distance and intimacy, weaving together the detailed gardener's art
with the natural background, taking advantage of the concept of "borrowed scenery."
Here the Moon Bridge and the Garden's plantings are softly surrounded by the hillside.

(Jerry Stelmack photograph)

The Antique Gate—at the base of a hillside of "borrowed scenery"—marks entry into the sanctuary that is Portland's Japanese Garden. This old structure sat in boxes for years after it was shipped from Japan. It was erected in 1976 as the magical entry to the whole Garden. The stucco walls were added later.

(Allan Mandell photograph)

A WORLD OF ITS OWN: ENTERING THE GARDEN

Vine maple leaves.
(Duncan Neilson, Jr. photograph)

Each weekday morning, often as early as 6:30 in the summer, head gardener Michael Giusti and his crew of gardeners enter the Garden. With no tools in hand, they are there to judge what needs to be done that day by each of the crew. Giusti says, "the Garden is kind of calling out for you." Their "stroll" focuses their attention on the landscape, and readies them for the steady and demanding maintenance required by such a large garden. Giusti says: "You look at it and you slow down."

Later in the morning, the public begins to arrive at Portland's Japanese Garden. There are two ways of entering from the public parking lot at the base of the hill. In the summer, at regular intervals, a small shuttle bus winds up around a high hillock and disgorges visitors at the Entry Gate. Those hardy persons able to take the short, steep hike up to the Garden enter through the Antique Gate at the base of the hill. This lovely structure was selected for the Garden by Professor Takuma Tono and purchased by the Japanese Ancestral Society. It sat for years awaiting erection after it was shipped to Portland. Tono had wanted this century-old structure to act as a gate to the long-planned pavilion in the Flat Garden area, however, with that building's construction delays, it was finally decided that, before

The sign that announces in both English and Japanese Portland's internationally known and admired Japanese Garden.
It was placed in its landscaped location adjacent to the Garden parking area in 1985.

(Allan Mandell photograph)

it rotted in its storage boxes, the Antique Gate should be made into the entrance to the whole Garden. In 1976, without any blueprints to guide the way, it was re-assembled in its present location. In 1990–91, the stucco and tile-topped walls were added by the Garden staff.

Approaching and entering the Antique Gate begins to prepare the visitor's mind for the whole Garden experience. Immediately, one enters into another world, sequestered, settling and calming. Walking up the winding five-hundred-foot path, the visitor first notes the roof end-tiles set into the walkway, and the ancient marker stone originally used on the old road from Kyoto to Edo (Tokyo). Nearby, where the path curves to meet the hill, is a water basin in the shape of a lotus blossom; for some years it stood where Professor Tono placed it as part of the water source next to the Tea House.

At the high end of the pathway, opposite the Entry Gate, looms an area honoring William deWeese, who gave a quarter-century of leadership to the Garden. The plantings on this sharp-sided hillock were designed and landscaped by former Garden landscape director Hoichi Kurisu, a long-time friend of deWeese's. Excepting those at the base of the hill, which came from the Timothy Lake area near Mt. Hood, all the stones and all of plants here came from the former Board president's personal garden. After his death in 1988, his widow, Kuniko deWeese, and two sons, Alexander and Douglas, donated it all to the Japanese Garden.

The stone paving at the Entry Gate is Belgian block at one time used to cobble the streets of Portland. These were recycled from the 22nd Avenue viaduct in northeast Portland, during the construction of the I–84 freeway. (This same stone can be seen as a demarking and detailing design element along the downtown right-of-away of Portland's light rail Max system.)

The Entry Gate, where each visitor pays admission and enters into the Garden proper, was completed in late 1966. It was designed after the traditional temple or shrine gate, called a "guardian gate," and is in the *daimyo* style. In pre-modern Japan, these *daimyo*-style gates were found outside the homes of feudal lords; they housed the men who acted as sentries. The larger, taller middle doors accommodated warriors on horseback; the doors on either side were for persons on foot.

The hand-made tiles on the gate's roof are from Japan. More than twelve tile shapes are required for authentic roofs, and they can be found not only on the Entry Gate, but also on the Tea House and the Pavilion. The peak and end tiles are called *onigawara* or demon tiles. These tiles keep evil spirits from inhabiting these buildings.

Outside, a large red pine stands sentry at the gate. Inside, two stone lions grace the Entry Gate. Normally, the lions would stand outside a temple, male at the left (with the orb under its paw), female on the right (with its paw protecting a cub). However, we live in a different world from the time of their original use. In order to protect them from being stolen, these lions have been placed inside the gate, thereby possibly losing some of their protective power. These *koma inu do*, however, still watch over the welfare of all who visit.

During the winter of 1996-97, the Garden repaved the area in front, through and beyond the Entry Gate, replacing rough Belgium block with smoother granite for better handicapped access to the site. A wider wheelchair ramp was added just inside the entrance.

On the back corner of the gate, there is a lower shingled roof designed to protect persons standing at the inside window of the entry office; it is made in the shape of a samurai's hat.

The visitor to Portland's Japanese Garden now stands poised at the start of a special journey, a unique experience, the Garden itself. Here

Mileage marker from the ancient road between Kyoto to Edo (now Tokyo). Since the opening of the Garden, this stone has greeted visitors. At the start of the entry trail, it symbolically sets the tone for the journey.

(Allan Mandell photograph)

The Garden House was constructed
from Alaskan cedar in 1986-87.
This building is central to the business
of gardening, the myriad activities
required of the gardeners.
Garden vehicles, tools and equipment
necessary for maintaining the Garden's
beauty are stored here.

(Allan Mandell photograph)

is where each begins to sense what is in store during the brief minutes or long hours ahead of them. As one Garden volunteer guide has noted: "This Garden is both remote from and related to the city of Portland." Having paid the admission, the visitor becomes at once a guest and invariably stops, pauses, looks around to decide where to go, and "strolls as if they have all the time in world."

The Garden is symbolic, but not in the literal sense. It is symbolic in a personal and individual sense. Each person gives to and takes from the Garden what each needs. The journey is as important as the destination.

The coast pine (*Pinus contorta*), just inside and to the right of the Entry Gate, is now a century old. More importantly, this tree has been pruned and nurtured for over sixty-five years. Pines in Japan are often attributed with courage for their stature and longevity; some allege that pines can live for a thousand years. However, that strength is best enhanced with careful pruning and shaping of these trees.

Just across the walk inside the Entry Gate is the water basin area, its stones placed just right for a calming act of cleansing. There should always be such a basin at an entrance. It is here that the visitor symbolically washes before entering into the garden experience. The water basin was hollowed from a stone selected by Tono. (This basin uses regular city drinking water; the streams and ponds throughout the Garden use re-circulated non-potable water.)

The three Ilex trees to the left of the water basin came from nearby Washington Park. They are now over fifty years old, and were untrimmed and unpruned before they were planted. The solid profile they once had has been changed to the more traditional shapes now evident. The three trees represent a father, mother and child.

Splendid examples of carefully pruned *kuromatsu*, or black pines (*Pinus thunbergiana*) give definition to the entrance area. The

HUMAN NATURE

three black pines represent "the matchmaker, the groom and the priest," for the bride had nothing to say in traditional Japan with the arrangement of marriage. Azalea, camellia, and viburnum complete this ensemble. The Japanese maples behind this arrangement and across the view toward the right were recently rescued from an area that was being developed at Portland's Oregon Health Sciences University. Here, as elsewhere in the Garden, there is a daily and seasonal dynamism, reflecting the changing foliage of the maples against the dark pine background, the bare nature of the deciduous trees during the winter, and the varied greens of the blooming shrubs after they have lost their brilliant flowers.

Walking toward the Strolling Pond Garden, the visitor passes the Gift Store and public rest rooms and (facing this new building) a handsome shore pine. Ahead is the Wisteria Arbor. The Garden's Antique and Entry gates are boundary gates. However, each of the interior gates in the Garden has, as Tono has pointed out, "a definite relationship to its surroundings. There is no break between inside and outside of the ground" at these gates. This is true of the Wisteria Arbor, so placed to frame the view of the Sapporo Pagoda Lantern (*goju no to*), and to draw the visitor further into the Garden.

Wisteria (*fuji*) is often used as a single plant in a tea garden. The Portland Garden's four plants that carry themselves across this gate are Chinese wisteria. These arbored plants are vigorous and the gardeners must trim them of many suckers during the summer. The surface under the gate is again recycled Belgian block removed from the surface of Portland streets.

The French white lilac (*Syringa vulgaris* 'Vestale') to the left of the Wisteria Arbor was planted in the early 1980s in memory of Hugh Shogren, a subtle remembrance of a city gardener who worked at the Garden for many years.

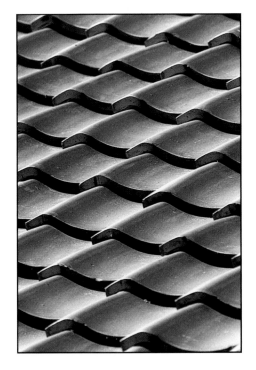

Each of the Garden's structures is roofed in the traditional manner, with tiles from Gifu, Japan. This detail is of tiles on the Garden House roof.

(*C. Bruce Forster photograph*)

Native Oregon vine maples (Acer circinatum) that were planted in recent years along the
wall near the Entry Gate. These small trees give the approaching visitor
a seasonal hint of what will be seen inside the Garden proper.

(Allan Mandell photograph)

HUMAN NATURE

(above right)
A view east from inside the Entry Gate.
Added about in the early 1990s, these
fifty-year-old Japanese maples now
bower the once open walkway.
(William Robinson photograph)

(above left)
Entry or "Guardian" Gate.
Fashioned after those outside the
homes of Japanese feudal lords.
(Deon Reynolds Photograph)

(below left)
Entry Gate during a 1977 snow storm.
This old coast pine is braced against
the weight of snow and ice.
During an ice storm the previous year
this tree had not been supported,
and it had been bent to the ground.
(William Robinson photograph)

The Garden is protected by guardian lions (koma inu do).
These symbolic animals traditionally watch over the welfare of all who visit a temple.

(C. Bruce Forster photograph)

Passing under the twisted and gnarled wisteria, the Garden's guest now stands at the center of Portland's Japanese Garden. All of the individual gardens in a sense spoke off from this hub site.

To the right is the Camellia Tunnel, where the pleached—interwoven—plants arch over the trail that leads toward the Moon Bridge and the Strolling Pond Garden. Small blossomed, these camellias are thinned out just after their spring blooming and are pruned lightly three or four times a year.

Further to the right of the tunnel, is a half-hidden walkway (to the upper pond) made of stones chosen by Professor Tono in 1965 at an eastern Oregon ranch near a Gilliam County settlement aptly named Lonerock. These small boulders have been used as stepping stones throughout the site, most notably on this path down to the Peace Lantern at the edge of the upper pond.

But what captures one's attention here is the striking, eighteen-foot Sapporo Pagoda, carved from stone quarried at Shikoku Island, a gift from Portland's Japanese sister city, Sapporo. It was originally located on the grounds of the Sugawara mansion in the Hokkaido city of Otaru, at the time the residence of Sapporo's Mayor Yasaku Harada. Harada donated the two-ton pagoda to the City of Portland in 1963, during a "cold April visit" to Sapporo by Portland Mayor Terry Schrunk and a delegation of Portland civic leaders. The nearly century-old pagoda already had been designated a "Japanese treasure."

The Sapporo Pagoda is called a *goju no to*, or five story tower. The five stories represent the five-fold elements, colors, cardinal virtues, and the five elementary forces. The nine rings at its top stand for the Buddhist concept of nine heavens. The crowning lotus blossom represents Buddha. Though called a pagoda this structure also serves as another of the Garden's stone lanterns.

The stones leading across the open space before the Sapporo Pagoda were removed from Dodge Park on the Sandy River, a stream that rushes from the western flanks of Mt. Hood into the Columbia River just east of Portland. These stones represent the island of Hokkaido; the red stone from Terrebonne, Oregon, on the left of this group represents the capital of Hokkaido—Sapporo. The large standing stone, which Tono placed to balance the whole arrangement, was brought from the Clackamas River, a major tributary of the Willamette River.

Tono designed the hedging behind the Sapporo Pagoda, integrating those variously trimmed shapes with the low profile maple to help move the eye from the ground up to the top of the pagoda.

As one walks down toward the lower Strolling Pond area, a large slope tends off to the left through the tall firs and cedars at the entrance to the Natural Garden. This is the Specimen Maple Grove, which was started with several plantings in 1995; more are to follow.

Already audible is the curiously affecting syncopation of the clacking bamboo Deer Chaser—or Deer Scare (*shishi o doshi* or *sozu*). (The original Deer Chaser was built by Professor Tono in 1964 and placed near the Tea House.) It is part of an arrangement (designed by former landscape director Takao Donuma. It is placed at the base of the large cedar (*Thuja plicata*), grand fir (*Abies grandis*) and Douglas fir (*Pseudotsuga menziesii*) trees at the intersection of the Cherry Hill path and the path to the Natural Garden. In 1986, the Buried Shaft Lantern (*ikekomi gata*), and the Japanese rice mixing bowl completed this attractive assemblage.

Facing the Entry Gate is a water basin. The is the place to wash symbolically before visiting the five gardens. Unlike the streams and ponds elsewhere in the Garden, this water is potable.

(Allan Mandell photograph)

(above left)

Blooming Chinese wisteria and
Hino crimson azalea

(Allan Mandell photograph)

(above)

Stone pathway to the upper pond.

(Bruce Lellman photograph)

(below left)

View through Wisteria Arbor.

(William Robinson photograph)

HUMAN NATURE

The imposing
Sapporo Pagoda
Lantern, a gift from
Portland's Japanese
sister city.
This carved stone
structure is the hub
of the Garden.
(Ron Cronin photograph)

View across the upper pond of the Strolling Pond Garden. The Moon Bridge, foliage
surrounding the connecting stream to the lower pond, and the background
of "borrowed scenery" complete this autumn scene.

(Ron Cronin photograph)

WATER & LAND: THE STROLLING POND GARDEN

Iris blossom.
(Jerry Stelmack photograph)

Descending the hill, left of the Sapporo Pagoda, the visitor pierces the arch of Cherry Hill. Trees extend from the near left across the greensward toward the Moon Bridge upstream. Many of them are *Yoshino* cherries (*Prunus x yedoensis*), the same as the world-renowned ones that circle the Tidal Basin in Washington, D.C. At the immediate left is one of only two examples of mahogany-colored ribbon bark cherry trees (*Prunus serrula*) in the Garden. The other is next to the white azalea hill above the upper pond. These trees, also called satin bark or birch bark cherries, are notable for their remarkable tiered surface. Its compelling tactile quality forced the gardeners to move it away from the path; formerly close at hand, visitors touched it so often (some, in fact, tearing off its bark) that there was concern about its survival. Just above it is a large, single, white *Tai-haku*—Japan's most popular cherry.

Two large pools, and a lovely running stream that connects them, are the centerpieces of the ambling Strolling Pond Garden. Through the concept of hide and reveal, this garden draws you to its ever-changing vistas; every few steps on each of its paths brings to view fresh and enchanting observations.

The strolling garden, developed from the influence of Chinese boating gardens, is one of the three major styles of Japanese gardens

View upstream toward the upper pond.
Shown is the original Moon Bridge.
One of the first structures built
(in the early 1960s). It was replaced by
the current bridge in 1990.
Heavily pruned, sixty-year-old
Japanese holly (Ilex crenata) and
Japanese skimmia (Skimmia japonica)
frame both sides of the stream.

(Rick Schafer—American Landscapes—photograph)

found today. Strolling gardens can be characterized as hill or pond style. These gardens have become the dominant landscaped form in Japan, and might be considered the most aristocratic style. Professor Tono suggested that these gardens came into their own during the Kamakura period (1186-1334) in Japan.

First called "go-around" pond gardens, their design became more sophisticated and compelling over time. These ponds, while made by human hand, have been carefully landscaped and tended to lend them a sense of naturalness. Tono wrote that:

> walks around the pond. . . permitted the varied angles at each step along the walk. So the shape of the pond was the principle factor receiving careful study. Portions of the boundaries of the pond are purposely obliterated by shrubs, trees or stones, to indicated undefined expanse and to add mysterious grandeur.

The Strolling Pond Garden contains all the elements that make up a Japanese garden: streams, ponds and waterfalls; stones and bridges; pathways and a wide variety of plants. It is the place where the landscaping techniques of borrowed scenery, captured alive, and hide and reveal all come into play.

Here one can stroll across a bridge or circle part of a pond. Running water, sometimes with a stepping-stone crossing, courses though the landscape. It is here that irises bloom annually in June. Landscaped hillocks, often made from the earth scooped to form the ponds, give relief to the views, and contribute to the mystery of hide and reveal.

Whether circling the upper pond, or standing on the Moon Bridge, or looking across the koi-filled lower pond toward the

Heavenly Falls, a Garden visitor finds an internal dimension that is balanced between the intimate and the grand. Using the available terrain as best as possible, and faced with limited resources, the plan for the Strolling Pond Garden incorporated the old zoo's aviary into the upper pond; the bear grotto became the lower pond, where the colorful koi swim. The Heavenly Falls cascades from what was the bears' winter hibernating den. (The koi—which also hibernate during the winter—have always been a delight to children, who often consider the sighting of these colorful carp as the high point of their visit to the Garden.)

The creation of the Garden required the trucking in of a substantial amount of dirt to cover the broken (and ugly) stone of the bear pit; much of the hillside beyond the lower pond has foliage now fully rooted in that trucked-in soil. For the ponds and the stream between them, more than twenty tons of stone were transported from the Sandy River near Ramona Falls, on the western slope of Mt. Hood. In addition, over eighty tons of stones were brought in from the Shell Rock Mountain area of the Columbia River Gorge.

Professor Tono wanted to use exclusively stones from the Columbia Gorge's Eagle Creek, stones he felt most nearly like those used in Japan. However, William Robinson (head gardener with the city parks department) and Forest Service personnel were opposed to taking so much stone from the pristine site, and allowed removal of only one load. According to Robinson, Tono said that, if it had been in Japan, all of Eagle Creek's stones would have been removed to private gardens.

The two large stones protruding from the pond's surface symbolize a tortoise on the left and a crane on the right. Both animals stand for long life to the Japanese. Stones representing this pair of

Heavenly Falls issues forth from what was once the Portland Zoo's bear hibernating den. It flows into the lower pond of the Strolling Pond Garden.

(David Whetstone photograph)

(above)

Today's Moon Bridge from east.

(Jerry Stelmack photograph)

(above right)

The upper pond from Moon Bridge

(Rick Schafer—American Landscapes—photograph)

(below right)

Moon Bridge from North Path.

(Ron Cronin photograph)

(below)

This small falls was added in 1983.

(Jerry Stelmack photograph)

Amidst an amphitheater of "borrowed scenery" is this autumn view from the Moon Bridge,
showing the stream connecting the two bodies of water in the Strolling Pond Garden.
On the right, is a light green Red Japanese maple (Acer palmatum 'Sango kaku').
On left is a purple leaf maple (Acer palmatum dissectum 'Atropurpureum').

(Steve Terrill photograph)

animals can also be found at the base of the cascades that tumble down the east hillside into the upper pond.

The Heavenly Falls provides an aural and visual backdrop to the lower pond. Looming over the falls are tall deciduous Japanese saw-leaf zelkovas (*Zelkova serrata*), often mistaken for elms. Selected as the background for the falls and the lower pond, they soften the hillside's otherwise strong evergreen and alder-maple mix of borrowed scenery.

Where the visitor stands contemplating the Heavenly Falls and the koi-filled lower pond, underfoot are seven large stones placed in the pavement; they represent the Big Dipper.

At the northwestern edge of the pond, carefully placed among the many large boulders that characterize this Garden, stands a Snow-Viewing Lantern (*yukimi doro*), another of the six lanterns originally chosen for the Garden in 1965 by Professor Tono. This style of lantern is so named because it shows its best under a mantle of snow. It has a rare eight-sided fire box, which reflects an older form of these popular lanterns; modern snow-viewing lanterns are generally six-sided.

In 1966, the Harp Tuner Lantern (*kotoji doro* or *kotoji gata*) was carefully placed, one foot on land, one foot in the stream flowing through this section. Always placed as a link between water and land, to symbolize their interdependence, the lantern's bowed legs give rise to its name, for its shape is likened to the tuning bridge on the Japanese harp—the *koto*.

Walking along the stream that connects the two ponds, the visitor may sense that the running water "initiate[s] a dialogue through the garden." Professor Tono wrote of the value of running water:

> A stream is always a pleasing sight in the Japanese garden, wherever fresh running water is available. It is customary to

introduce the stream in a very naturalistic manner. A stream is . . . often constructed to take the form of a serpentine course or of a "Inazuma gata"—lightning pattern.

The stream connecting the two Strolling Pond Garden pools, has been softened over time by the careful planting and pruning of the hundreds of plants along its course. The main path below the Moon Bridge is bowered spring and summer with maple trees. The thread-leaf cypress (*Chamaecyparis pisifera* 'Filifera') that stands near the Harp Tuner Lantern was planted in 1973.

Tono's design of the Strolling Pond Garden quietly integrated, another element that he felt important to a representative Japanese garden: the viewing pond garden. While these Edo period (1600-1868) gardens were made to fit in small urban settings, with a commanding view from a building, Tono gave this garden a similar view from both the fenced edge of the pond and from the Zigzag Bridge. All the elements of the garden: waterfall, stream, pond, garden hill—are arranged to be seen from the viewing spot. Wrote Tono: "The capricious irregularity of natural water scenery and conventionalization of the layout were thoroughly studied and the resemblance of natural beauty was always created."

Another approach to the lower pond is by way of the appealing and magnetic Zigzag Bridge. The carefully designed structure was built by Hachiro Sakakibara, extending Tono's earlier structure. Sakakibara diverted part of the main stream, and added the recycled granite steps from the Civic Auditorium to the trail leading to the bridge. Some contend that this indirect bridge pattern is designed to protect those who cross it from demons, who must travel in straight lines. Whatever the origins, this kind of bridge assures that the stroller takes a measured pace. As one moves through the combination of plants, most particularly ferns and irises planted alongside,

each turn of the bridge offers an insight and a new vista. As one approaches the lower pond via this bridge, the foreground plants and the larger view in the background seems to bring out the depth of the Garden. An exploring desire emerges, a desire to see more.

Although Professor Tono originally planned to plant the irises near the Sand and Stone Garden, the iris beds were planted in the Strolling Pond Garden in March–April 1967; they bloomed almost immediately that June. Over five hundred rhizomes were planted by gardeners Hugh Shogren and Kinya Hira, among them choice *ensata* or Japanese flat iris (*kaempferi*) variety. The iris beds were redesigned by Hachiro Sakakibara at a later date. The flowering of these lovely plants annually coincides with an *ikebana* show at the Garden. The plants are trimmed back each November, and about every five years the rhizomes are removed and divided. (The extra bulbs are often sold or given away to members of the Garden Society.)

Best viewed from the Zigzag Bridge are two arrangements of hardy water lilies—planted in place of water hyacinths (*Hyacinthus orientalis*) which became too invasive—set off in two stone-encircled sections of the stream. These plants bloom in the spring, and are never touched or dealt with in the same manner as the irises.

The cherry blossoms in the small orchard above the lower pond come into bloom each year in late March. The *akebono* (daybreak) cherry now seen there was originally planted near the Sapporo Pagoda; Tono replaced it with a low-lying cut-leaf maple at a later date. These trees were hit hard by a "silver thaw"—a severe ice storm—in 1979.

Americans have a very different view of walking safety compared to the Japanese. Nowhere is that more evident than in the absence of true stepping stones in this Garden. The original crossing downstream from the Moon Bridge was made of twelve-inch thick stepping stones from eastern Oregon. However, to assure good footing and safety for Garden visitors, those stones were replaced by smooth rectangular granite slabs from Portland's old Civic Auditorium.

Stepping stones appeared in Japanese tea gardens first. As with other great Japanese garden designers, Tono understood the need for exacting arrangement of stepping stones:

> The line of stepping stones is usually beautiful, consisting of small flat stones, arranged as though by the hand of mother nature herself. . . . Their practical use is desirable but they must be combined with beauty for artistic appearance. The whole layout is arranged in studied irregularity for both comfort in walking and artistic effect.

Just west of this lower crossing of the Strolling Pond Garden stream is a lovely tall stone, a viewing stone, which was brought to the Garden from Shell Rock Mountain in the Columbia River Gorge. (Viewing stones are placed in a garden where the visitor is assured of a special place to observe the scenery.) This stone is the same type as the stone used for the Buddha in the Sand and Stone Garden.

Beyond the Moon Bridge is the upper pond, the largest body of water in the Garden. The dominant plant at the upper pond is a large weeping willow (*Salix babylonica*) that softly drapes itself over the northern edge of this substantial body of water. (Another, diseased, willow hovered over the opposite side of the pond until it was removed in 1995.) A companion willow stands near the upper side of the lower pond. Gardeners often thin out the willows during the spring and summer months.

The two statuesque bronze cranes permanently residing on the upper pond's western shore were gifts from the Bank of Tokyo, pre-

Portland's Japanese Garden
uses "borrowed scenery"
to set its five gardens
in a larger context.
Here snow-covered evergreens,
mostly Douglas firs,
form wintery enclose of the
Strolling Pond Garden.

(C. Bruce Forster photograph)

Where the slight scrim of ice
allows, the upper pond's
snow-covered shoreline, background foliage and its weeping willow are doubled in the
smooth reflecting waters.

(C. Bruce Forster photograph)

Winter scene at the lower pond of the
Strolling Pond Garden, with the
Snow-Viewing Lantern, swimming koi
and Zigzag Bridge.

(C. Bruce Forster photograph)

The two-footed Harp Tuner Lantern
(with one foot in the water, one on land)
stands between the two great ponds of
the Strolling Pond Garden.

(C. Bruce Forster photograph)

The lower pond of the strolling Pond Garden. Sitting on its own moss-covered peninsula the
Snow-Viewing Lantern adds a human touch to this portion of the Garden.
An Acer palmatum offers its yellow protection to the lantern,
and stone crane emerges from the pond's surface.

(Ron Cronin photograph)

36   HUMAN NATURE

A blossoming Kwanzan cherry tree
and a dwarf red camellia
are part of the short-lived burst
of spring color on the
Garden's Cherry Hill.
Beyond are the lower pond, Heavenly
Falls, and the Snow-Viewing Lantern.

(Steve Terrill photograph)

An autumnal view
(from behind the Sapporo Pagoda) of
the Garden's Cherry Hill.
Best known for their spring finery
of pink and white, these trees
also produce lovely fall colors,
here seen through the framing boles
of great evergreen cedars.

(Ron Cronin photograph)

*Quietly flowing down the eastern hill
above the upper pond
is a small waterfall.*

sented on the occasion of the opening of a branch of the bank in Portland. These stately birds—the only metal statues in the Garden— stand amidst stones (*suhama*) that represent a beach. Individually chosen from Indian Beach at Ecola State Park on the Oregon coast by vacationing William Robinson, these matched, dark stones represent a sandy shore surface—a "beach garden." Professor Tono has written that "seashore rock is always used along the water-edge of a pond or a lake." "Water stones" like these are extremely valuable in Japan.

Subtly tracing through the White Azalea Hill that rises toward the outer stucco wall north of the upper pond is a "dry falls," with stones to represent water. The white azaleas were planted in 1969 (around several delightful small maples) in honor of the Garden Society's first president, Philip Englehart. Englehart was particularly fond of these snow-blossomed plants, which he had seen on one of his journeys to Japan. The azaleas came from cuttings grown at the city greenhouse near east Portland's Mt. Tabor (a small extinct volcano, now a city park), which can be seen from the viewing area east of the the Garden's Pavilion.

In contrast to these dry falls, a small waterfall on the upper pond's east side splashes into the water. Its rippling sound and movement counter and juxtapose the serene and quiet surface of the pond.

Bridges in Japanese gardens do carry persons over water, but they have their own aesthetic and function. "The Japanese conception of a garden bridge is not by any means that of a passage over water, instead it is the love of picturesqueness or sometimes a fondness for enjoying the cool breezes and watching the fish below," wrote Professor Tono.

The Western redcedar Moon Bridge, with its bronze lotus buds (*giboshi*) capping each railing post, is probably the public's favorite viewing spot for the Strolling Pond Garden. It most certainly is the linking visual element between the two portions of this area. The *giboshi* were produced by Japanese craftsmen especially for the Garden. Heavy use and the elements wore on the original bridge and a replacement was constructed in 1990. The century-old boxwood tree (from the grounds of St. Mary's Academy) stands across the path from the western end of the Moon Bridge.

At the southeastern side of the upper pond, and best seen from the west across the pond, is the Peace Lantern, a *Yukimi* or snow-viewing lantern, which resides in its second home in Portland. The curved legs of this lantern are called *neko ashigata*, or "cat's claws." There is special power and poignancy to this lantern's history and its name. It arrived in 1954 on the first merchant ship from Japan to Portland after World War II. A gift to the City of Portland from Yokohama, it was placed with great care in Washington Park's International Rose Test Gardens. At that location, several hundred yards below the Japanese Garden, this lantern, with its inscription, "Casting the Light of Everlasting Peace," was ironically subjected to repeated vandalism; the crack in its roof, the umbrella (*kasa*), is now covered with moss. In 1967 the Peace Lantern was placed permanently in the Strolling Pond Garden.

For many years, the east slope above the upper pond, just below the recently built gift shop and rest rooms, was hidden in a stand of ungainly junipers. In 1985, this hillside was improved with the planting of vine maples, pieris, and kalmia. After the disruptive construction period when the gift shop was built, new stones, cedars and maples were added to fill in this area.

The Strolling Pond Garden surrounds the Tea Garden, which sits nestled against the steep western hill above the site. These two very different layouts, with different purposes, here, in Portland, are most companionable neighbors.

A post-war gift to Portland from the Japanese city of Yokohama, the Peace Lantern (which is one of several snow-viewing lanterns throughout the Garden) sits poised on the eastern shore of the upper pond.

(William Robinson photograph)

Reflected in the still waters of the upper pond is the Japanese Garden's traditional Tea House. Constructed in Japan, it was taken apart and rebuilt on this site for a 1968 dedication. The gate (at right) was added two decades later.

(Ron Cronin photograph)

CEREMONY & RITUAL: THE TEA GARDEN

Lace-leaf maple.
(Jerry Stelmack photograph)

Bringing a calm Buddhist cohesion to the Garden are the Tea House and Tea Garden. Places of quiet and reflection, tea gardens are often composed of inner and outer sections, carefully placed stone pathways, lanterns, a site for cleansing with water and water for the tea ceremony, and a tea house.

Tea gardens are the one Japanese garden form that require a building. Never residences, tea-houses are meant for the performance of the formal tea ceremony (*chanoyu*), using special bitter, powdered green tea known as *matacha*. In what is known as the *sukiya* style, these "simple and relaxed" small buildings have a rough-hewn aspect about them, a "refined poverty" brought about by "profound artistic forethought."

Since impermanence is a major Buddhist concept, these buildings are built of basic, simple, but carefully selected natural materials that are by definition fragile. Unfinished posts and earthen walls, all befit the simple tea ceremonies that take place within their confines. These ceremonies, through their emphasis on quiet, ritual, and timelessness, induce a tranquil serenity, a peace.

Japanese Buddhist priests who studied in China brought back to Japan the habit of drinking green tea, which was first grown along the Yangtze River. Because meditation comprises a major component of

(above)

Walk in outer Tea Garden. Both the outer and Inner gardens were rebuilt in 1984.

(Janet Loughrey photograph)

(left)

This graveled pathway through the Strolling Pond Garden courses along the eastern boundary of the Tea Garden.
In the distance is the gate that allows visitors to have a close-hand view of the Tea House.

(Jerry Stelmack photograph)

HUMAN NATURE

The Viewing Stone (right) stands at the granite walkway into the outer Tea Garden.
The walk's stones were once part of the steps at Portland's old Civic Auditorium's entrance.
Along with azaleas and Japanese maples, there is at the right a Mugo pine
(Pinus mugo var. mugo) just showing the new growth of its candles.
Some time later the gardeners will snap these off to retard growth.

(Janet Loughrey photograph)

The outer Tea Garden's Guardian Stone. The ground cover is New Zealand brass buttons (Leptinella squalida) that has the look of miniature ferns.

(Allan Mandell photograph)

Buddhism, the use of tea held off drowsiness for the priests. Seeds brought back from China around the twelfth century, and planted near Kyoto, made that city a green tea growing center.

The tea ceremony's ground rules were established in the fifteenth century, founded on the concept of "the spirit of calm and sobriety" —called *wabi*. As the ceremony was developed, so was born "tea taste," an aesthetic philosophy that extolled the beauty of a single flower displayed in the decorative alcove (*tokonoma*). Tea taste "embraced rustic simplicity and restraint."

Tea houses are made up of several strictly defined sections. There should be a service or anteroom (*mizu ya*) where the utensils for the ceremony are readied beforehand. The actual sitting room (*zashiki*) is where the tea ceremony is performed. In addition to the *tokonoma*, there are subsidiary alcove with cabinets, interior sliding screens (*fusuma*) that act as partitions, and the exterior (*shoji*) screens. There are mats (*tatami*) on the floor. Japanese rooms are described by the number of *tatami* they contain. The standard number of *tatami* for the tea house is four or four and one half.

The tea house should be set in its own garden; the tea house garden is considered one of the three main garden styles found in Japan today. Tono remarked that "the garden must look natural, so made to arouse sensations in harmony with the sprit of the tea ceremony and conducive to a meditative frame of mind. Once in the garden, one may feel detached from the world and away from the hustle and bustle of life." Guests are asked to wait at a portico (*machiai*) in the outer garden (*soto roji*). (Another structure, not found in Portland's Japanese Garden, called the "waiting room"—*yori tsuki*—is often used.) Whilst waiting, the invited ones are able to take time to calm themselves in preparation for the ceremony.

The first structure in Portland's outer tea garden is the old

HUMAN NATURE

machiai, set against the steep hill that makes up the western border of the Garden. Just north of the *machiai* is a solitary evergreen, *Cryptomeria japonica*, a tree used for timber in Japan. Directly across from the *machiai* is a short seven-ringed pagoda, or Spirit House (called by some *hokyo intoh*), set amidst the shrubbery. Not a lantern, this pagoda is part of the symbolic and prayerful meaning of this garden, something for the tea ceremony guests to see as they wait. One of the original six "lanterns" chosen by Professor Tono in 1965, this small structure is not complete; part of it was stolen.

When they are to enter the tea house, guests are led through a gate and along the "dewy path" (*roji niwa*) through an inner garden (*uchi roji*). Portland Garden designer Takuma Tono wrote that:

> since this garden assumes a passage style, the arrangement of stepping stones is very important. In passing slowly from one stepping stone to another, with the garden swept and watered most scrupulously beforehand, the guests cannot remain indifferent or unsusceptible to the beauty of nature enhanced by the art of the landscape gardener.

Behind the inner garden's wall near the traditional *machiai* is a bamboo fence and a "dive-in-gate" (*nakakurguri mon*), a split bamboo door banded together with cord that swings up, which is purposely designed to cause all to bow as they pass through—a symbolic way of producing equal status among all who participate in the ceremony. The gate was built by Kichiro Sano. Next to the gate is one of the maidenhair (*Ginkgo biloba*) trees in the Garden.

Since the inner garden (*roji*) is closed to the public, entry into the Tea Garden grounds is from the northwest corner of the Strolling Pond Garden, by the upper pond. Through a gate at that location, and to the right, is a second *machiai*, which has been placed here in

The diminutive and appealing Spirit House gives its blessing to the outer Tea Garden. Native Pacific Northwest moss surrounds its base.

(Janet Loughrey photograph)

(above left)

Tea House from the water basin.

(Allan Mandell photograph)

(above right)

Tea House exterior.

(Allan Mandell photograph)

(below left)

Small sleeve gate near the dustbin.

(Allan Mandell photograph)

(above)

Long sleeve gate bears the weight
of a new snowfall.

(Allan Mandell photograph)

(above left)

The Portland Garden's Tea House.
The long sleeve gate
is in the foreground and open shoji
and fusuma screens reveal
the zashiki, or sitting room,
the place of the tea ceremony.

(Deon Reynolds photograph)

(below left)

The view of the Tea Garden from the
interior of the Tea House. The tatami
mat seating area is where the tea
ceremony is performed.

(Allan Mandell photograph)

*The inner garden has two lanterns,
one of which is the ikekomi gata or
Round Post.
Beyond its lighting function, this style
is used for a variety of other purposes:
offerings, repose, burial and even as
decoration.*

(Janet Loughrey photograph)

order for visitors to have a restful view across the full Garden. This *machiai*, the entrance gate, and the new walk to the back of the Tea House, were built in 1984.

Plantings in the Tea Garden are not showy, for nothing should detract from the calming aspect of the whole ritual. Often there are lanterns to illuminate the way. Tono wrote:

> the introduction of stone lanterns. . . seems to have an intimate relationship with the tea [ceremony] . . . . The reason that the lanterns were used in the garden was perhaps to illuminate the ground and to guide the guest walking on the stepping stones and washing their hands before going into the tea room during the nocturnal tea ceremony.

In most cases any surrounding fences and hedges should be high, in order for the intimate nature of the tea ceremony to be contained within the inner garden's limited vistas. In the case of Portland's Tea Garden, the hemlock hedge (situated on its low Belgian block wall) has been purposely trimmed low to afford a view across the Strolling Pond Garden and hilly area to the east, and to allow for a view of the closed inner Tea Garden from the Strolling Pond pathway.

When the Tea Garden's inner and outer areas were re-landscaped, a new trail was added behind the Tea House on the west hillside to afford visitors a better view of the closed-to-the-public inner garden. For safety reasons, that trail was subsequently closed. In 1995, a new bamboo fence, bound with the traditional winding pattern, was placed between the inner and outer gardens.

The serene Tea House (*chashitsu*)—now nearly thirty years in place—was designed by Professor Tono, assembled in Japan, fully pegged, dismantled, carefully marked, and shipped to Portland, and re-assembled using almost no nails by a Japanese carpenter from the Portland area. (The Tea House sits where the Portland zoo's coyote pens were once located; its grounds are made up of thirty truckloads of topsoil deposited there in 1971.) The Tea House roof tiles are from Nara.

This rustic structure was dedicated on 1 June 1968 with a tea master from Japan performing the ceremony. Since that time, numerous public demonstrations of the tea ceremony have been performed at the Tea House.

At two of the Tea House corners are bamboo "sleeve gates" (*sode-gaki*), so called because of their resemblance to kimono sleeves. One of the few lilacs in the Garden stands between the sleeve gate and the water basin. This plant, a Japanese tree lilac (*Syringa reticulata*), was part of a gift from the Sapporo Snow Festival Queen during her visit to Portland in 1963. Just outside the Tea House's entrance hidden behind the small sleeve gate is a dust box, which has both literal and symbolic uses (a place to deposit what is swept up; a place that one puts away spirits that might prove contrary).

Near the smaller sleeve gate, on the south side of the Tea House, is the gathering of elements (lantern, water, basin, stepping and kneeling stones) that constitute the water source for the tea ceremony. Part of that assemblage, are a Christian Lantern (*oribe*) and a water basin at its foot, both carved from Shikoku Island granite. (The original square lotus blossom basin—*masugata tsukubai*—has been replaced by this oblong water basin.)

The style of lantern was named for Furuta Oribe (1543–1615), a noted early tea master and warlord, who was also Christian. Since his western religion was frowned upon by the leaders of Japan, its symbolism was stylized. It is suggested that the figure at the lamp's base is

Located next to the Tea House is a water basin, with stones for kneeling and placing of utensils.
This bouldered gathering is designed to provide water for the tea master prior to the tea ceremony.
The light source is a Christian (oribe) Lantern.

(Allan Mandell photograph)

*Sitting almost unnoticed
next to the bamboo covered water well
(with its traditional pulley)
is this delightful Movable Lantern.
Symbolic of lighting the water source,
this pumpkin-sized lantern
is covered with native moss.*

(Janet Loughrey photograph)

the Virgin Mary, and that the rotund section at the top of the base is a stylized cross. As with *ikekomi gata* in the Natural Garden, and the example next to the Deer Chaser, the *oribe* is a buried shaft lantern.

Lending further traditional order to the arrangement of lantern and basin are specially placed stones. During the course of the tea ceremony, the tea master must come to the bamboo spout for the water. As with all parts of the ceremony, there needs to be a graceful way of doing this. Stones specifically chosen for their purpose and size are placed adjacent to the basin to ensure this; here: to the left is a *teshoku seki* stone; to the right a *yuto seki* stone, both of which are placed for Tea Ceremony preparation purposes. At the front is a larger, flat stone on which the person kneels during this part of the ritual. The basin itself is purposely low, assuring a stooping position and the humility required by the ceremony.

Stone wells were often alternative water sources for the tea master. In this Tea Garden there is one in the outer section. The bamboo covers are merely decorative. Near the outer garden well is the "Movable" or "No Legs" (*oki doro*) Lantern, which is portable because of its size. This now moss-covered delight was one of the original six chosen by Professor Tono.

The Tea Garden is truly a garden within a garden. Everything has its purpose in this serene layout. All the exterior plantings and placements are directed toward making the Tea Ceremony harmonious and precise. Excepting days when it is simply too cold to have the screens open, the tea ceremony in the Tea House does not turn its back on its surroundings. They are an integral part of the ritual, and quietly surround it with all the sanguinary effects that such a garden can produce.

With its pulley
and bucket held by a
rustic post and arm,
this bamboo-covered
well in the outer area
of the *Tea Garden* is
arranged in the
traditional manner.
Some wells have a
small, protective roof
over the
pulley apparatus.

(David Whetstone photograph)

This gate was built to afford visitors to the Garden a close-hand look at the Tea House,
while protecting the outer and inner portions of the Tea Garden from heavy pedestrian use.

(Janet Loughrey photograph)

HUMAN NATURE

(above)

Maple at the new Tea Garden gate.

(Janet Loughrey photograph)

(above right)

Old machiai in the Tea Garden's outer area.

(Janet Loughrey photograph)

(below right)

Walkway and new Machiai.

(Allan Mandell photograph)

This hillside cascade brings life and activity to the calm and sequestered pond
in the Natural Garden. The hillside above, guarded by tall Douglas firs,
its rocky face softened by azaleas and rhododendrons,
is often mirrored in the pond's still waters.

(Ron Cronin photograph)

DESIGNED CHAOS: THE NATURAL GARDEN

An understood human control of nature, a precision, is typical of a Japanese garden. A balance, a carefully controlled—a trimmed—nature is the more common hallmark. However, Portland's Natural Garden gives the visitor a seeming chaos, plants conforming to more ragged and un-controlled shapes, it would seem. Despite its appearance, this kind of garden has the daily touch of the gardeners; that touch is used to bring about a chaos that is controlled.

A long, gently sloping walk, leads from the Sapporo Pagoda area to the Natural Garden. Along the ground, a carefully detailed stone drainage flue, brings the eye to one of the mysteries of the Garden. A small bas-relief figure (the only human form in the Garden) has been carefully placed at the base of the left hillside sloping down from the mid-1990s addition to the Garden, the Specimen Maple Grove. This figure—called a *jizo* statue—was found one day in the Tea Garden, left there by an anonymous donor. Representing the *Bodhisattva*, who was to watch over people after the death of Buddha—Japanese *jizo* represent a kindly and protective deity.

This area was originally planned and developed by Professor Tono as the Moss Garden (*koke niwa*); it opened in 1968. (This Garden's plants—aralias, hepaticas and ferns—were described at the

A Deer Chaser, Buried Post Lantern and a rice bowl form an ensemble located between the Natural and Strolling Pond gardens. Its sound echoing throughout the Garden, the Deer Chaser sits sheltered under cedars and firs.

(Allan Mandell photograph)

Anonymously donated to the Garden,
this Bodhisattva of unknown origins
peacefully watches over the entrance
path to the Natural Garden.
It is an impressive reminder,
despite its modest dimensions
and the rough wear,
of the religious associations these
gardens have in Japan.

(Allan Mandell photograph)

time in the *Oregonian* as "happy plants.") Tono was probably inspired by the famous moss garden of Saiho-ji in Kyoto. After a flood and fire in the fourteenth century, mosses and overgrown trees gradually took over the grounds; eventually giving the temple on the grounds the name Koke-dera, the Moss Temple. Tono's version, had just the opposite origins, for it was a garden designed on purpose. The Moss Garden was built in a matter of days during one of Tono's trips to Portland. Though it was supplied with indigenous mosses from nearby Mt. Hood, this Garden proved almost impossible to maintain. Despite elaborate efforts to mist the mosses and intense maintenance, birds and rodents were attracted to the site, and their digging and rooting ruined the garden.

In the early 1970s, the landscape designers Hachiro Sakakibara and Hoichi Kurisu made substantial changes to this garden. Sakakibara added a pond (which still carries the appellation, "Saka's Pond"), the third largest in the whole Garden. The two gardeners planted azaleas, pieris, pines and other plants, and placed some of the recycled Civic Auditorium granite steps along the walkways and stairs. They forged the shape of what is now called the Natural Garden.

In some ways this is the most intimate of the five Gardens. Symbolic of the spiritual journey of each life, this is a place where the visitor is enclosed in an envelope of plantings, running water, views that change with each step—where the Japanese concept of hide and reveal works so well. The walkways and the stairs bring new, intimate, views at every turn; little bridges bring the cooling rush of water to a close proximity. There are bowers, and some views almost alpine.

It also is a space that reflects the journey of life through the seasons, for deep changes are wrought as the year passes. This Garden is the most changeable—most affected by the seasons—of all of the gardens: the dazzling flourish of spring color; summer's peaceful enfolding of greenery; the sudden, open view of streams, boulders, and bare outlines of trees and shrubbery after the fall's glorious leaves are lost; winter opens up the scene with a mountain feeling brought by snow on this steep hillside site.

The entry path passes through the moon gate—so named for the small half moon and the larger full moon doors, which makes a distinctive asymmetric gateway. During the full moon the wider side of this split gate is left open; the crescent or new moon is matched by opening the narrower side.

 The visitor will note a difference in terrain. Left behind is the more gentle, moss-covered slopes that surround the long walk to the Natural Garden's gateway entrance. Immediately through the gate the hillside site steepens, giving the whole setting a strong wilderness feel about it; a dense set of trees, shrubs, and other plantings come into view. On the slope above the Natural Garden's waterfall near the Tombstone Pagoda (*shoto*) is an old, grafted maple that was given to the Garden in 1964 by Gerald Avery.

 At the base of the falls in "Saka's Pond" there is a stone representing a carp swimming upstream. Nearby, on the far shore of the pond, is the petite Mushroom Lantern (*oki doro*). Barely a foot high, this lantern symbolically guides boats to their safe refuge at the end of a day.

 Three bridges in this Garden characterize the variety of ways that persons are carried across running water. At the lower end of the pond there are two substantial structures made of granite blocks rescued from the remodeling of Portland's old Civic Auditorium.

The Tombstone Pagoda, a 1965 gift from the Minobu Buddhist Temple near the Japanese town of Kofu. It is a carved five-tiered pagoda, with an image of Buddha on each of its four sides. These handsome carvings traditionally denote a grave or a sacred spot.

(Janet Loughrey photograph)

(above left)

"Saka's Pond" and falls.

(Ray Atkeson—American Landscapes—photograph)

(above right)

The entrance to the Natural Garden is the Moon Gate.

(Allan Mandell photograph)

(below right)

The jaunty Mushroom Lantern.

(Janet Loughrey photograph)

HUMAN NATURE

(left)
Pedestal Lantern.
(Janet Loughrey photograph)

((above, right
Azumaya from steps above.
(William Robinson photograph)

(below right)
Mud or Sod Bridge. White Everest azalea in background.
(William Robinson photograph)

(above)

Korean Snow-Viewing Lantern.

(Janet Loughrey photograph)

(above right)

Square basin is a turn-of-the-corner
surprise in the Natural Garden.

(Bruce Lellman photograph)

(below right)

Moon tiles at the lower gate.

(Janet Loughrey photograph)

(above left)
**Steps from the Azumaya to the
Sand and Stone Garden in the autumn.**
(Jerry Stelmack photograph)

(Above)
Same steps from in the spring.
(Allan Mandell photograph)

(below left)
Natural Garden stream.
(Allan Mandell photograph)

One of the delights of the Garden are the surprise emergences of lanterns as one wanders through the five gardens. Meticulously placed, they seem natural in their chosen spaces. This is the affecting Buried Shaft (Ikekomi) lantern.

(Janet Loughrey photograph)

There is a beguiling choice of two paths in this garden. Off to the right, is the "road less traveled," a lower path leading toward the Waterscapes section of the Garden. At the junction of the stairway between the two Natural Garden trails is an easy-to-miss low-profile Buried Shaft Lantern (*ikekome-gata*) huddled under rhododendrons. Placed in this location in 1974, this charming, friendly piece was another anonymous gift to the Garden.

The Waterscapes form the lowest portion of the whole Garden. Entry here is via a temple-style gate—added in 1987. Its thick shingling gives the feeling of a thatched roof. Symbolic full and crescent moon tiles are embedded in the pathway at the gate. Located just inside of this split Gate of the Full and Crescent Moon is the Garden's Korean Snow-Viewing Lantern (*yukimi gata*). (Believed to be Korean in origin, it is a type commonly seen along the coast of the Sea of Japan on the main island of Honshu.) Just beyond is a small pond, once a reflecting pool, now with a splashing waterfall and a surround of small trees.

The tile-roofed *azumaya*—the "waiting building"—is a perfect place to sit, rest and reflect, to enjoy the "distance" this simple structure has from the Garden as a whole. This perfect place, a spot of scent, sound and coolness, is a resting spot before resuming the stroll back to the upper levels. Resting in the *azumaya* offers an opportunity to study the Crescent Moon Lantern (*eitokkuji*), one of the newer lanterns in the Garden, with its moon and sun carvings.

The *azumaya* (as with the two *machiai* in the Tea Garden) constitutes as close to a garden house as any building in the Garden. Professor Tono commented that "a garden house in the Japanese garden is nothing like that of the English garden. A naturalistic, rather rustic type house meets our taste more than the elaborate or finished style of the western garden." As the visitor climbs the hillside pathway leading away from the *azumaya*, that person will be surrounded by hundreds of azaleas planted in memory of Hugh Shogren, the city gardener who worked with the Japanese Garden for years. His "hillside garden" is a spring-time visual joy.

Further along on this path joining the walkway from the pond, the sojourner passes over a subtle arch that represents a soil, sod or earthen bridge (*do-bashi*). East of the *do-bashi*, and above the inviting staired descent into the Waterscapes area, is an old Pedestal-style Lantern (*zendoji*). One of the older lanterns in the Garden, it is styled in a rustic texture, and has a different deity carved in each of the four sides of its firebox. Rarely used as a light source, this kind of lantern is important for the Buddhist message it conveys.

As visitors move eastward, they make the most radical transition in Portland's Japanese Garden; exiting the designed chaos of the Natural Garden to emerge in the spare and simple beauty of the Sand and Stone Garden. In some ways this transition also honors the remarkable dual influences of Shintoism, with its naturalistic side, in the former garden, and the more austere Buddhist exemplar in the flat, walled expanse of sand and stone in the latter. It is yet another example of the remarkable ways Portland Garden lends itself to suprise.

The Crescent Moon Lantern
sits next to the Azumya
in the Natural Garden.

(Janet Loughrey photograph)

Late afternoon sun plays on the carefully raked surface of the Sand and Stone Garden.
Here the base of the Buddha Stone seems to ripple concentric rings
across the Shirakawa sands.

(Bruce Lellman photograph)

ZEN SEVERITY: THE SAND & STONE GARDEN

During the warring medieval period of Japanese history, when the power of the ancient imperial court declined and growing military control took its place (the era that has been the stuff of so many Japanese samurai films), there was little time for continued development of architectural styles. One place that this did not hold true was in the Zen Buddhist monasteries where monks developed new designs for gardens. Among them was the "dry landscape" (*karesansui*).

Best exemplified by the now world-famous Ryoan-ji temple garden in Kyoto, with its fifteen stones seemingly scattered in its Shirakawa sand, these gardens are open to as many interpretations as there are viewers who behold them. Sand and stone gardens are usually small in size with a surrounding low earthen wall. The sand, usually fine gravel, replaces water in other traditional garden styles, and the stones stand in for trees and mountains or other objects.

Not only was the *karesansui* garden radically different in its materials from traditional water and plant gardens, but the method of viewing it was also a departure. It is unlike many sites with large ponds or lakes, which might be viewed from a boat as in the Heian-era gardens. And it is unlike the Chinese parks. So much of the early inspiration for the gardens came from China, and in the Heian peri-

Sand and Stone Garden edging of Gifu roof tiles and small Oregon coast stones capture wind-driven needles, leaves and bamboo.

(C. Bruce Forster photograph)

The Sand and Stone Garden from the view area of the Flat Garden. This Garden is one in which absorbing silence, and the implication of movement, bring the viewer into its visual hold. It is by design flat, affording no overview within its confines.

(C. Bruce Forster photograph)

HUMAN NATURE

This garden stands unchanging during the year, with its stationary stones and surrounding sand. Yet, a winter snow fall brings a new look—softening, almost hiding, the raked patterns—and brings a new sense of surface to the Sand and Stone Garden.

(C. Bruce Forster photograph)

Bamboo grows next to
the tile-crowned wall surrounding
the Sand and Stone Garden.
Bamboo has
a strong association with Japan,
yet its role in gardens can be limited.
In Portland's Japanese Garden
its use is spare and precise.

(C. Bruce Forster photograph)

od—an age when significant Chinese culture imports were imbued with uniquely Japanese attributes. It is unlike the strolling gardens of the Edo period. The *karesansui*, the abstract Zen garden, is meant to be seen and contemplated from a single stationary point—a place to meditate and to be meditated upon.

These are gardens where the inner meaning of nature is displayed, rather that the more obvious externals shown in the other types of gardens. These are intensely personal places where the impulse to silence is encouraged.

Portland's Sand and Stone Garden, unlike the Ryoan-ji, is not overwhelmed with thousands of visitors; disgorged from dozens of filled tour buses, led by guides using bull horns to squire their charges through an overly visited sanctuary, the Ryoan-ji is often a most un-Zen-like place. Portland's Zen garden, on the other hand, has the advantage of relative quiet.

The *karesansui* can produce a mysterious feeling, brought about by the unique, and profound, Japanese cultural perspective. Though permanently stationary, the stones in this kind of garden can and do give the sense of movement amidst the sea-like sands that surround them.

The only foliage found in these gardens is usually moss at the base of the stones, or moss that naturally finds itself on the tops of the stones. Of course, trees and other foliage outside the low walls often contribute to the total effect of the garden—the contrast of green pines can make these gardens more striking. Professor Tono felt that materials used in such a garden "are not changeable but beautiful and the quiet atmosphere is most desirous."

Unlike botanical gardens, which are often representative of nature in a more compact form, the spare spaces in Zen gardens are used to represent other places, things or animals. They are often likened to islands in the sea, a natural response to countless island-dotted locations in the Japanese archipelago. Some have been thought to represent certain stellar constellations; the Ryoan-ji garden has been thought to represent Cassiopeia. Many times stones can be interpreted as animals—herons, turtles, or others—depending on the stones chosen.

While it is suggested that it is best to avoid literal interpretations of the stones in this kind of garden, the eight stones in this garden are arrayed to portray a Japanese story:

> A tigress wished to determine the valor of her seven cubs (the smaller stones in the garden, from near Wapanitia Pass southeast of Mt. Hood). She decided that to do so she would force her offspring into the waters of the sea (the sand surrounding the stones), as a test of courage. The Buddha (the large stone, from Shell Rock Mountain in the Columbia River Gorge), who feared for the survival of the young tigers, dove into the sea. The cubs survived using him as sustenance, "symbolizing the infinite compassion of the Buddha for all forms of life."

The sand in this Garden is the same used at the Ryoan-ji garden in Kyoto; it comes from the Shirakawa River near that old Japanese imperial city. In 1994, new Shirakawa sand replaced the material that had been in place for thirty years. Washed and revitalized, by the Garden's staff, it was melded with the sand in the Flat Garden for added depth. Both gardens now have renewed material for the lovely patterns raked in by the gardeners. A gardener raking these intense patterns must follow the admonition given by a Ryoan-ji monk: "Don't think or your lines will not be straight."

A Demon Tile caps the end
of the tile-topped stucco wall
surrounding the
Sand and Stone Garden.
Made on the Japanese Island of Gifu,
these traditionally shaped tiles are
found at the roof-ridge ends
of the Pavilion, Azumaya, Tea House,
Entry Gate and Gift Shop.
They protect the structures they guard.

(Janet Loughrey photograph)

(right)
The Sand and Stone Garden in a later manifestation.
In 1994 moss-covered earthen surrounds
were added to the stones in the Garden,
an example of the continuing changes
found daily in the Japanese Garden.

(Allan Mandell photograph)

(above left and right)
For years, since it was first developed under Professor Tono's direction, the Sand and Stone Garden's Buddha
and seven companion stones stood directly in the sand.
With the arrival from Japan of new Shirakawa sand in the mid-1990s,
the arrangement was altered slightly, each stone given the added dimension of moss-covered berms.

(Allan Mandell photographs)

HUMAN NATURE

The tiles protecting the top of the wall surrounding the Garden are from Nara, Japan. The stones supporting the wall's base are originally shaped for the famous old Columbia Gorge Highway. Five truckloads of cut stone were removed from the old highway when what is now I-84 was under construction.

Persons who find it hard to navigate the steep stairs to the Sand and Stone Garden can enjoy the striking and stark space from a special viewing site just south of the Pavilion in the Flat Garden area.

The long range
of composite material steps
that ascend from the Sand and Stone
Garden to the Flat Garden.
Here the visitor skirts the bowered
Natural Garden,
to emerge in an open area
dominated by the Pavilion.

(Bruce Lellman photograph)

One of the singular trees in Portland's Japanese Garden is this striking, century-old, lace-leaf maple that provides seasonal changes just off the Pavilion's west verandah. It is the second maple at this position.

(Ron Cronin Photograph)

LAND & SYMBOLIC SEA: THE FLAT GARDEN

Lace-leaf maple and post.

(Jerry Stelmack photograph)

P rofessor Takuma Tono, the Garden's designer, wrote: "In Japan, when a man comes home from work, no matter how small his garden, he should take off his business jacket and put on his Japanese coat, pour a cup of sake and walk in his garden and relax and contemplate. Only then should he join his family."

The style of garden most often contemplated by the homecoming businessman is the flat garden. Although the flat garden is one of the earliest manifestations of garden design in Japan, it is a form not usually found in American versions. According to Tono, flat gardens are mostly found in confined areas in cities, making this Garden's example unusual in its expansiveness.

As Tono suggested, "the monotony of the [flat] garden is relieved by stones, trees, stone lanterns, a well or water basins and stepping stones." The Portland Flat Garden contrasts grass and moss, along with plantings of evergreens and flowering azaleas, all balanced against white Shirakawa sand, the arrangement's raked centerpiece.

Professor Tono exerted much of his early attention on the Flat Garden. The process started in earnest in 1962, with grading of the area and, in 1963, the building of the Stone Bridge, made of boulders brought in from the Wapinitia area southeast of Mt. Hood. Tono insisted on dense plantings around the sand portion of this Garden.

Haloed by the green camellia leaves
and vivid red blossoms,
the Garden's Olympic Lantern
stands at the long bend
of the inner trail
of the Flat Garden.

(C. Bruce Forster photograph)

This density was criticized by some accomplished Portland-area gardeners. However, Tono wanted to have a full garden as quickly as possible—to give a "complete show" almost at once. He knew as these trees and bushes matured they would be culled. Over time, gardeners would adjust and move plants. That delicate human touch would keep the plantings in balance, and mean that the Garden would be ever changing. Despite the fact that the original planting was done under his direction (following his plant layout), when Tono revisited the Garden he had many of the plants in the Flat Garden re-sited. They had been seated too low in the ground, he decided they needed to be raised above the "sea level" of the sand.

Not everything was done right the first time in the Flat Garden. It is on the site of the old zoo's primate cages. (The Pavilion rests on what was a parking lot.) The cages were on a small hillock, which Tono had graded. Four feet of earth was removed to make it level with the parking area. Since the Shirakawa sand had not arrived, a unfortunate blinding white crushed rock from near Ashland, Oregon was temporarily used during a brief early public viewing of the Garden. Photographs from that time reveal that bark dust had been used around the plants, and traditional American park benches were placed here and there.

Walking back toward the Gift Shop from paths out of the Natural and the Sand and Stone gardens, take the graveled inner path that veers off to the right. This pleasant foray takes the visitor past a variety of maples, pines, a large redbud tree (*Cercis canadensis*) on the left, some wonderfully pruned Hino-crimson azalea, and the Olympic Lantern. This *Kasuga*-style lantern is so named for the Olympic Rings carved into its top. It was the gift of Dr. and Mrs. Walter Lobitz, Jr. in 1979. Carved in Sapporo, the lantern originally had been given to them by the Japanese Dermatology Association—hence the "1964 JDA" inscribed on it—in recognition of Dr. Lobitz's acclaim in Japan.

The visitor's path will then lead to the massive, round and flat-topped stone steps to the western verandah of the Pavilion. These boulders were brought to the Garden from Mt. Hood's McNeil Forest Camp vicinity, near the headwaters of the Sandy River—removed with full approval of the Forest Service.

Standing on the west-side verandah on a rainy day, the visitor will notice why the Japanese Garden went to the effort and expense of choosing just the right sized Shirakawa sand; for even in the heaviest rains, this sand holds its carefully raked designs. At least once a month a gardener re-rakes this expanse, often with a new pattern, reflecting mood and impulse at the time.

There are two trees that dominate the near view of the Flat Garden from the west-side verandah: a cut-leaf maple to the right, and a weeping cherry at the left. The large Japanese lace-leaf maple (*Acer palmatum* 'Dissectum Atropurpureum') at the north side of the raked sand, is actually the second such tree placed at this location. The original donated tree, one of the first plants placed in the Garden, died in 1971; the current one is a century old.

The Garden's one large weeping cherry (*Prunus subhirtella* 'Pendula') commands the southern side. Wary of this plant's dominant shape, Professor Tono allowed only one in the Garden. It was salvaged during construction of one of Portland's freeways.

Amidst the seascape sand portion of this garden are two shapes—a gourd and a sake cup—made up of low-growing plants and dramatically laid out island-like in the sand. Originally ruby dianthus formed these "islands," but its bright-pink color proved too intrusive; they are now composed of woolly thyme (*Thymus pseudolanuginosus*), plants that better segue into the total layout of

The gray of the Garden's Poetry Stone offers beautiful contrast to a rhododendron ('Jean Marie de Montague'). White coloring highlights the incised characters that translate: "Here I saw the same soft spring as in Japan."

(C. Bruce Forster photograph)

(right)

*Spring brings a profusion of color
to the Flat Garden's inner trail.
Along its graveled reach,
the Garden visitor will find
flowering bushes and trees,
and the Olympic Lantern,
all underscored with
soft-colored native mosses.*

(Janet Loughrey photograph)

(right)

*The Pavilion's tile roof
from inner trail.
With its dedication in 1980,
Professor Tono's
dream that Portland's garden
should have a primary building
was brought to reality.*

(Allan Mandell photograph)

HUMAN NATURE

The Flat Garden's Inner trail's approach to the Pavilion.
The vivid yellow-green leaves of a redbud tree centers this view.
Hino crimson azaleas show their immaculately trimmed shapes in the foreground.

(David Whetstone photograph)

*Yuki zuri are used each year
to support the branches
of Garden pines vulnerable
to the weight of snow and ice.*

(Allan Mandell photograph)

this garden. These two forms connote pleasure; spiritual and temporal. The circle, which represents the sake cup, also has deep Buddhist significance of enlightenment. The gourd represents happiness.

Southwest across the sand portion of the Flat Garden is a bridge built from stones brought in from Bear Springs near Mt. Hood. One of the first elements placed in the Garden by Professor Tono, it was erected during four extraordinarily wet days in November 1963. Near the bridge is a maple brought to the Garden in 1965 from Dodge Park along the Sandy River east of Portland.

The enormous flat stone, to the right of the gourd, was brought to the Garden under the supervision of landscape director Masayuki Mizuno and William Robinson in 1979. The stone, most of which is buried, was lifted (with much drama and near disaster) from the Hood River during a two-hour extraction. Beyond the time and danger of its move, and because of its size and shape, this stone has been called the most valuable one in the Garden.

On the next tongue of "land," a Wet Heron Lantern (*nure sagi*) sits elegantly amidst trimmed azaleas. It is a superb choice for a Portland site, for the blue heron is the city's symbolic (and official) bird. This lantern, which is said to represent the sacred bird standing in fields with dampened feathers, is best seen from the Pavilion's western deck.

In mid-December, about the time of the Winter Solstice, and before the traditional time of Oregon's heavy snows, the gardeners place several striking rope-and-pole structures around the Flat Garden. Known as *yuki zuri* (snow guard), these conical devices—"golden spider webs of ropes" and poles—support limbs on trees prone to collapse under the weight of snow or ice. Winter-time visitors best see the *yuki zuri* from the west verandah of the Pavilion, where trees surrounding the Flat Garden stand shored up with these

HUMAN NATURE

lovely shapes. (In Japan, when gardeners work with tall pines, the ropes are often tied directly to the trunk of the tree instead of a pole. These are called *miki-zuri*.) *Yuki zuri* have come to represent winter to the Japanese, and hence have a seasonal decorative function.

Representative of the way Japanese have made beautiful even the most utilitarian objects, *yuki zuri* are but one of several devices that protect plants from undue weight or too much sun, or that train plants with rope: many bamboo and rope braces help the gardeners train tree limbs to keep them from lifting too high—as limbs naturally tend to do; braces can protect branches from snow or ice breakage; pyramidal supports called *takemata* (bamboo forks)—can be seen under branches, bracing and training trees into specific shapes; numerous burlap-wrapped plants seem bundled against the elements, for burlap (which eventually rots away) protects trunks from sunburn, or after transplanting.

At the south end of the west verandah of the Pavilion is a stand of black bamboo (*Phyllostachys nigra*) at the left of the steps. Another grouping of this lovely form of Japan's ubiquitous plant can be found at the east side of the Tea House.

The large blue-green Iyo stone off the southwest corner of the Pavilion, is from a province of the same name in Shikoku. A memorial honoring the original president of the Society, Mr. Philip Englehart, this eight-foot stone, which weighs two tons, is most striking—showing off its variegated bands of green, gray and black—when dampened by rain or mist. (Professor Tono thought the "color of stone" was of great importance, equaling that of its shape.) It sits behind a low bamboo fence, amidst a sea of pebbles.

Across the path that circles the whole upper level of the Garden to the south of the Iyo stone is a fine view of the Sand and Stone Garden; this viewpoint also operates as handicap-access viewing site.

(above and below)
Bamboo trains young pine's limbs and a Japanese snowball plant (*Viburnum plicatum* f. *tomentosum*).

(Allan Mandell photographs)

(above left)

Viewed from the west verandah
of the Pavilion
is the Garden's grafted weeping cherry
(Prunus subhirtella 'Pendula').
It spreads its hulking—yet delicate—shape
at the edge of the raked sand area.
It was recycled to the Garden in 1963, saved
from freeway construction.

(William Robinson photograph)

(above right)

Emerging from the brilliance
of spring-flowering shrubs
is the Wet Heron Lantern
(from west verandah).

(Janet Loughrey photograph)

(above)

The Pavilion has a large central room,
whose glassed doors offer view toward
the city and the mountains to the east,
as well as the more intimate view of the Flat
Garden across the west verandah.

(Ron Cronin photograph)

HUMAN NATURE

(above left)
The eaves, railing and floor
of the Pavilion's west verandah
frame the large lace-leaf maple,
the Garden's most photographed tree. In all
seasons, this striking plant, so carefully
cared for by the gardeners, enthralls visitors.

(Bruce Lellman photograph)

(above right)
Brilliant Hino Crimson azaleas,
with their crafted shapes
contrast with with boulder stairs
to the west verandah
of the Pavilion

(Bruce Lellman photograph)

(above)
The Flat Garden's photogenic
lace-leaf maple
seen from the inner trail.
Here it is in the spring-time transition
between flowering and leafing.

(Bruce Lellman photograph)

Situated near the popular overlook
of the city of Portland,
and southeast of the Pavilion,
is the Contemporary Lantern.
Its design is in striking contrast
to all the other Japanese lanterns
in the Garden.

(Allan Mandell photograph)

Here can be found the Poetry Stone. The English translation of the Japanese inscribed on this stone: "Here I saw the same soft spring as in Japan." A line of carefully pruned Scots pines (*Pinus sylvestris*) stretch along the crest of the incline into the Natural Garden.

The areas south, east, and north of the Pavilion are designed as extensions of the Flat Garden, though the most unified section is that west of the building.

In 1988, to honor the Garden's twenty-fifth anniversary, Portlander Don Wilson sculpted a drinking fountain paid for by the City of Sapporo. It was dedicated in late July 1989 (the thirtieth anniversary of the sister city association between Portland and Sapporo), when Sapporo's Mayor Takeshi Itagaki visited Portland. The pines in this section are a mix of Scots and Japanese red.

Across the path to the east of the Sapporo Plaza is a small planting area dedicated to the memory of Fred Gast; Gast was the Society's first treasurer. This sweet, subtle spot is notable for its grafted crooked-leaf maples.

In 1980, Mr. and Mrs. William Roberts donated the contemporary lantern (the *Kansyuji*—so named for the Kansyuji Temple in Japan) that stands near the flagpole at the southeastern border of the Flat Garden. It was made of granite in Okasaki, a small town near Nagoya, and placed in its current location before the Pavilion was finished.

East of the Pavilion is the Hirsch Viewpoint Garden, dedicated to Harold Hirsch, long a supporter of the Garden. It encompasses the gravel and granite area used each year for the annual Moon Viewing evenings; the Harold Hirsch Hillside, below the boxwood hedge; the cedar and bamboo fence along the eastern edge of the Garden; the small Hirsch sub-garden at the northwest corner of the Pavilion.

Hirsch is additionally honored by a splendid Stag Lantern (*kasuga gata*). Hirsch is German for "stag." The lantern was originally obtained in 1980 from a factory in the town of Okasaki. The *kasuga* is named for a famous shrine near Nara, Japan. The striking piece has firebox carvings of a quarter and full moon, as well as a snail and a deer. The latter are thought to be "divine messengers," and are well-known in the parks and shrine precincts in Nara.

The Garden's one "dancing peacock" maple (*Acer japonicum* cv. 'Aconitifolium' – Maiku jaku) shades this lantern. A swath of heavenly (sacred) bamboo (*Nandina domestica*) nestles around the maple, the lantern and the large chain that trickles water off the Pavilion roof. North of the lantern is a contorted lace-leaf maple transplanted from the grounds of a northeast Portland office.

The most dramatic example in the Garden of borrowed scenery is seen from the Hirsch Garden, where visitors gaze across downtown Portland to the stunning backdrop of the Cascade Range. This view has been enhanced by careful removal of limbs from the hillside trees around the eastern perimeter of the Garden.

The boxwood hedge that circles from the viewing point left and around the Pavilion is trimmed each year with a view toward what will be its final shape.

From the earliest meetings of the Japanese Garden Commission, and the first plan laid out by Professor Tono, there was a desire to have a main pavilion in the Garden. Tono's original pavilion plan was a more substantial building than the one finally built. His design featured traditional breezeways, and, at the northeast corner, living quarters for a live-in Japanese landscape director. However, time and time again, the efforts to plan, raise money and finally build such a structure were delayed. The Flat Garden, which was laid out from the

The handsome Stag Lantern
stands in elegant pose
next to the northeast corner
of the Garden's handsome Pavilion.
It was placed here
in the area honoring
Harold Hirsch.

(William Robinson photograph)

(above)

The Flat Garden as well as the Sand and
Stone area contain
the two sand areas in the Portland Garden.
The Flat Garden's expanse is
bounded by dozens of plants,
forming the shoreline of this sea-like design.
The gardeners rake various patterns
in it during the year.

(Bruce Lellman photograph)

(above)

Late afternoon autumn sun highlights
the raked sand pattern of the Flat Garden.
The Shirakawa sand gives emphasis to the
Wet Heron Lantern and beautifully trimmed
border plantings.

(Allan Mandell photograph)

HUMAN NATURE

(above)
A fiery, contorted lace-leaf maple at the
Pavilion's northeastern corner.
This lively plant almost leaps
with its convoluted trunks and branches.
Since it was brought to the Garden
as a mature tree,
the gardeners have made its shape more
remarkable and balanced.

(Allan Bruce Zee photograph)

(above)
The Iyo Stone stands at the southwest corner
of the Pavilion. Selected in the late 1960s
from stones found on the Japanese Inland
Sea Island of Shikoku, it was dedicated at
this spot in June 1968.

(Allan Mandell photograph)

LAND & SYMBOLIC SEA: THE FLAT GARDEN   85

In the fall of 1994, the Citrus Lantern was added to the Garden, situated at the northwest corner of the Pavilion.

(Janet Loughrey photograph)

very beginning of the Garden's construction, was designed to be viewed from a raised pavilion. Not until the building was finally completed in 1980, was Tono's goal reached.

Designed by Skidmore, Owings and Merrill architects David Pugh and Richard McBride, this structure emulates the Japanese style, while using western construction methods. The Pavilion's handsome wood is Alaska cedar, instead of the traditional Japanese timber tree, *Cryptomeria*. The roof tiles are from Gifu, Japan, and match those on all the roofed structures in the Garden. And, as with the recently built Gift Store, the roof has an understory of copper shingles. Though the building's floor is hardwood, its layout represents and area of ten sections of tatami mats, ten each to a section. Each tatami is six-by-three feet. The dark strips on the floor are six feet apart, a multiple of the three-foot mats. There are three sets of sliding door panels that open onto the two verandahs; each panel has three-level screening: outside wooden, then glass, then shoji. The east-side verandah—which affords the best view of Mt. Hood—is the stage for various Japanese events and occasions. The Pavilion was dedicated on 18 May 1980, the day that Mt. St. Helens erupted. Shortly after it was dedicated, the building received an award from the Portland Beautification Association.

Those responsible for the Garden have had a consistent policy governing the use of the Pavilion—restricted to protect the integrity of the Garden. Excluding such events as weddings, cocktail parties, and food service to the public, the Pavilion's main room was designed for Japanese Garden Society business, and special activities relating to the Garden, such as *ikebana* shows and tea ceremonies. Two offices in the building serve the Garden's administration; the kitchen is used for Pavilion events.

Former landscape director Masa Mizuno spent the day of the Pavilion opening on the western porch taking in the roof-framed view of the Flat Garden. Mizuno has said: "The Flat Garden was just right. The eye frames it and takes out the background trees. The vast extravaganza is the western view. So this Flat Garden works for both Japanese and American eyes."

Along the northern fence, west of the boxwood surround, are a number of trees, among them a *Sango kaku* maple.

As visitors exit the Garden, they will come upon an anomalous fixture. This is the Lantern-Style Firebox Cover, which was built in the style of wooden Japanese lanterns—it disguises a strategically placed fire hydrant. Though an absolute necessity to protect the valuable Garden structures, the hydrant would be a discordant visual intrusion. During visiting hours it is hidden within this cover. At closing time every day of the year, this structure is wheeled out into the walkway, so that quick access will be available if the fire department ever needs to handle an emergency in the Garden. The characters painted on the side state "Be cautious of fire."

Entry area Lantern-Style Fire Box.
Built to cover a necessary hydrant
during the hours the Garden is open.

(Jerry Stelmack photograph)

Considered one of the symbols of Portland's Japanese Garden is the Moon Bridge. This traditional structure, deciduous and evergreen trees, walkways are all elements of a traditional garden.

(Rick Schafer—American Landscapes—photograph)

DEDICATION TO GROWTH: A SHORT HISTORY

Entry area burning bush
(Jerry Stelmack photograph)

Early in the 1960s, when the Japanese Garden Society first planned to use the dilapidated and abandoned old Washington Park Zoo, an exchange student from Japan visited the empty, scoured, boulder-strewn site. There was little—almost nothing—to indicate what this place would become. That same person revisited the remarkably transformed Garden in the mid 1980s, and she shed tears over the transformation—the beauty of the place.

As early as 1959 (the year of Oregon's statehood centennial celebration, and only fifteen years after the end of hostilities between Japan and the United States) some Portland leaders—under the aegis of the Japan Society of Oregon—were conjuring ways in which to interest Oregonians in Japan, to "bring the Japanese culture to this area without mimicking." These persons were looking for a way to honor a century of Japanese-American relationships.

Among the many ideas on the table were the establishment of a sister-city relationship between Portland and a comparable city in Japan, as well as finding a suitable spot for a Japanese tea house. Since it was a new direction they were proposing to follow, there were (and would be) a number of odd turns and dead ends as each succeeding group of leaders worked their way toward the Garden we have today.

In 1959 the Japan Society of Oregon (now called the Japan-American Society of Oregon) formed a Garden Committee. Searching for a way to follow, the committee even debated whether they should push for a sand or vegetable garden.

These early leaders knew that substantial funds would have to be raised (the earliest estimated figure was $200,000) and a local landscape architect would need to be found. By 1960, the Garden Committee had set its sights on the West Hills site of the old zoo in Washington Park. That year, Japan Society members were calling for an independent permanent organization to be formed solely for the development of a Japanese garden in the city.

Almost at once they turned to the Portland Park Department, under Harry Buckley, and they shrewdly moved to involve Mayor Terry Schrunk. Schrunk, it turned out, would be a key player in establishing Portland's world-famous Japanese Garden. Schrunk already had initiated Portland's first sister-city association with Sapporo, on the northern Japanese island of Hokkaido, in 1959. Sapporo (called "City of Lilies of the Valley"), with a world-renowned winter festival, was a new and modern metropolis, younger than Portland (the "City of Roses").

According to the *Oregonian*, Schrunk "wanted to create trade relations with the Orient," and having a Japanese garden in Portland was one more way of strengthening that arrangement.

A Portland businessman, Don Bates, inspired by the increasing trade and cultural ties linking Oregon with Japan, was sure that Oregon should and must have a traditional Japanese garden. His enthusiasm in turn inspired Mayor Schrunk and several others and led a number of dedicated persons to form the non-profit society to build a garden.

In June 1962 the Portland City Council created the Formal Japanese Garden Commission. Mayor Shrunk wrote:

> This Garden will provide the citizens of Portland with an area of great beauty and serenity and at the same time represent a warm, understandable link with Japan.

From the outset, there seemed to be only one site considered. With the demise of the old Washington Park Zoo (replaced by what is known today as the Metro Zoo, in a new location nearby), the city was concerned about what to do with the old zoo property just above the International Rose Test Gardens. City Commissioner Ormand Bean was convinced (since the city "did not know what to do with the place") that the site offered the best spot for the development of a Japanese garden.

In a later memo about "good-will" relations between the City of Portland and Japan, Bates described the reasoning behind the Society's early determination to have the old zoo site to Mrs. Leith Abbott, a long-time Japanese Garden Board member:

> Some had visited . . . Gardens on the Pacific Coast and Eastern Seaboard. Not one offered the possibilities for development as did this particular site in Portland. Traditional buildings and the Japanese mastery of the miniature garden vistas presented in this spot a magnificent opportunity for Portland's citizens.

However, the zoo site was not a done deal, and in August 1961, Thomas Kerr wrote the Japan Society Garden Committee's chair, Thomas Young, that the Japan Society should "secure the services of a qualified Japanese landscape gardener to inspect the various sites available. . . in our existing city parks and then make a recommendation. . . as to the most desirable location." He also suggested that brief plans and a cost estimate should be made at the very same time.

When the Japan-America Conference of Mayors and Chamber of Commerce Presidents met in Portland in 1961, delegates came to the site of the present Japanese Garden for dedication ceremonies, and planted camellia bushes they thought had come from nineteen cities of Japan. (The donated plants were killed by gassing required by US Customs, and local plants were substituted.) The Garden had its official ground-breaking ceremony in September 1961. The actual dedication of the five-and-one-half acres site took place on 5 December 1962 by Mayor Schrunk, while Sapporo's Mayor Yosaku Harada was visiting the city.

In November 1961, at a meeting of the Japan Society in Portland, a non-profit "organization on planning and raising funds for a Japanese Garden in Portland" was formally proposed. City Commissioner Ormand Bean, a planning participant, proposed that the Garden should have a dollar-a-year lease similar to that for the Oregon Museum of Science and Industry (OMSI) and the new zoo. The City of Portland agreed to a ninety-nine-year lease of the old zoo site for the Garden, to be reviewed and re-issued every five years.

Mayor Schrunk, fulfilling his role on the Formal Japanese Garden Commission, wrote the city attorney on 13 February 1963, informing that office about the formation of the Japanese Garden Commission and that:

> In order that the project may move along as rapidly as possible, it would be my desire that the City Attorney's Office prepare a draft of a contract for this purpose patterned after the existing contract between the Zoological Society and the

City of Portland for the consideration of the Japanese Garden Society of Oregon.

While there continues to be cooperation on the part of the City of Portland, from the very beginning, no tax money has been specifically appropriated for the Garden.

The Garden's association with the city was constantly adjusted and tuned. While there was a cordial and trusting relationship, certain matters had to be treated with great care. All additions and improvements made to the Garden had to be approved by the city. At various times, the city allocated funds to support Park Bureau work on the Garden. Over the years, the Society has reimbursed the city for these and other charges. For example, on 30 April 1965, the city transferred of $5,500 from a trust account to the General Fund, Parks Maintenance Division for materials and supplies to be used in the Garden.

Members of the Commission were from the mayor's office, the city council, garden clubs, the Japanese Ancestral Society, the Japanese Consul's office and the Japan Society (the organization that had suggested the creation of a garden in Portland). Under the direction of President Philip Englehart, the first members of the Garden Commission were: Mrs. Leith Abbott, City Commissioner Ormand R. Bean, Mrs. Henry F. Cabell, Roland Davis, Mrs. Rosemary Frey, John Fulton (President, Japan Society of Oregon), Paul Hunt, Thomas Kerr, Mrs. Morris Schnitzer, Mayor Terry Schrunk, Mrs. Robert H. Shiomi, C.B. Stephenson, Tom Tamiyasu (President, Japanese Ancestral Society), the Honorable Katsuma Urabe (Japanese Consul), Ray Vester and Thomas Young.

The Commission almost at once officially changed its name to the Japanese Garden Society of Oregon, an appellation it retains to

(above right)

Imagination is required to conjure this
scene transformed into
the Strolling Pond Garden.
But it was imagination that fired the
early Japanese Garden leaders
to hire Professor Takuma Tono
to make the transformation
to today's idyllic setting.
In this 1940's view a group
(at the spot of today's Moon Bridge)
strolls along the one-way drive
that wound through
the old Portland Zoo.

(Japanese Garden Archive)

(below right)

The zoo's bear pit
is now the location of the lower pond.
The slope behind the parked cars
is now Cherry Hill.
Following Professor Tono's sketches,
Portland City Parks architect,
Ed Erickson, designed the ponds.

(Japanese Garden Archives)

BEAR DENS, CITY PARK, PORTLAND, OREGON.

this day. The first meeting of the Society took place in the conference room of the Park Bureau on 15 January 1963. During this period, the Board met at various sites around downtown Portland, and its small office in the Portland Chamber of Commerce Building grew with hand-me-down equipment and furniture.

Only a few weeks after the city attorney approved their contents, the articles of incorporation for the Japanese Garden Society of Oregon a non-profit corporation, were filed on 14 December 1962. Philip Englehart was the first chairman. Nine days earlier, Englehart and Commissioner Ormand Bean had supervised the removal—by bulldozer—of four feet of soil at the location of the zoo's old primate house in preparation for laying out the Flat Garden.

It took vision for those interested in creating a Japanese garden to commit themselves to the location; the abandoned zoo property was described as merely "a rock pile." William "Robbie" Robinson (head gardener with the city parks department), who worked on the Garden from the very beginning, noted in a newspaper interview in 1984 that he remembered the desolate area, five-and-one-half acres which had a sole Japanese maple sitting on the scoured earth where the zoo had stood. "I thought it was hopeless." Little did anyone expect the transformation that has taken place.

However, there was in the early planning stages of the Garden an attitude that paralleled what Japanese gardens are all about: "The Japanese attitude of focusing on the total picture and not a single thing—the long-term view." Planners did not expect the Garden to happen overnight.

As part of their "long-term view," Garden supporters had already contacted well-respected Japanese garden designer Professor Takuma Tono of Tokyo. In February 1962 the Garden Commission had announced that Professor Tono had agreed in principle to be the

In January 1963, this maple,
saved from a southwest Portland
freeway construction site,
was the first tree planted at the
Japanese Garden.
This view (looking west)of the
graded Flat Garden area
was taken in June of that year.
The tree was poorly planted,
set in what one gardener called
"a hollowed out bath tub"
in the clay soil.
It eventually died from sitting in water.
It was replaced by the brilliant maple
now seen from
the Pavilion's west verandah.

(William Robinson photograph)

Portland Japanese Garden's designer. Englehart and several others traveled to Japan in the fall of 1963; while there, they met with Tono to go over plans and Tono's contract.

In 1963, Tono was hired officially as the "designer and consultant supervisor" for the Garden; the contract was signed on 18 October. Tono, with a degree from Hokkaido University and one in Landscape Architecture from Cornell, had been the head of the Landscape Architecture Department at Tokyo Agricultural College. He had designed and constructed a number of gardens throughout the United States, including a recently finished commission at the Brooklyn Botanical Gardens in New York. The scheme for the layout of the Garden was the work of the remarkable mind of this single person.

On 10 April 1963, Harry Buckley wrote the Oregon State Board of Landscape Architect Examiners to approve a Japanese designer for the Garden, after word of Tono's arrival was issued in the press. The landscape board (understanding the necessity of using someone from Japan, outside the pool of registered landscape architects) had notified the Society of the need for a "temporary permit."

Tono produced several variations and sketches of what would finally be the general layout of the Garden. Among his early variations were different placement of the iris beds (he had them below the Sand and Stone Garden), at least two locations for the Sand and Stone Garden, and a "cable car" or tram to carry visitors up the hill to the Garden (Tono commented in 1963 that a number of gardens in Japan had such conveyances). The western hillside above the Strolling Pond Garden was once conjured by Tono as an azalea hill. With the exception of the added fifth area, the Natural Garden, Tono's final concept of four areas (Flat, Pond, Tea and Stone gardens) remains the backbone of the present Garden. Today, one is struck at how closely

One of Professor Takuma Tono's sketches for the Garden, sent to Portland in January 1963.
This sketch shows the Flat Garden viewed from the future Pavilion.
The sake cup and gourd have a prominent place, and there is a lantern
where the Wet Heron Lantern now stands.

(Japanese Garden Archives)

all the subsequent gardeners and designers have adhered to Tono's ideas.

The original cost estimate for bringing the Garden into being was $219,000, but it soon grew in excess of $300,000—an estimate submitted in March 1963. At the same time a dual fund-raising and membership drive was initiated.

President Philip Englehart had the Board meet at a box-lunch gathering on the site of the Garden in October. It was a fund-raising kickoff, and the president's call for "100 percent attendance" was typical of his frustration with some lackluster Board support. Along with his assiduous and daily fund-raising efforts, Englehart increasingly displayed a hard-pushing style. His driving, cajoling and enthusiastic early leadership would prove key to the early success of the Garden program. By March 1963, the Society had in its possession two carved stone lanterns, the first of more than twenty that would eventually be set carefully across the landscape of the Garden. About the same time Englehart was unsuccessfully looking for sand for use in the Flat as well as the Sand and Stone gardens.

Sand was not the only problematic material. Tono was to visit the site in the fall of 1963, and in preparation, Park Department Superintendent Harry Buckley, William Robinson and Edward Erickson traveled through Oregon's hinterland searching for stone to match Tono's scheme. In October 1963, Buckley noted that it was important that stones chosen for Japanese gardens are not quarried, so stones had to be found in their natural state. Buckley estimated that the parks staff logged over five hundred miles hunting for the right stones for Professor Tono's layout. They looked at examples along the Clackamas and Zigzag rivers, as well as up the Columbia Gorge, around Mt. Hood, and near Warm Springs. The result was 162 stones that arrived on flatbed trucks in the fall of 1963 in time for

Tono to place them. However, number 163, a special flat stone, still eluded them. Tono never was able to select this stone, although significant flat stones have been added to the Garden.

After much "digging, leveling and hauling of top soil into the area," a thousand plants were put in place. Using the varied topography available at the site—and moving nearly two thousand yards of surface dirt—the city garden crews quickly leveled the Flat Garden, tore out the old zoo's bear pit for the lower pond, scooped and graded the whole Strolling Pond area, poured the reinforced gunnite bed—nearly two thousand yards—for the two ponds and their connecting stream, and laid in the first of what would become hundreds of massive stones found throughout the Garden.

The Garden's first Japanese cut-leaf maple was donated by Mrs. Anna Kelly. John "Tree" Kelly (no relation) donated his time and equipment to remove the tree from her garden at sw Fifth and Carruthers, which was destroyed by construction for the I–405 freeway. Originally brought from Korea around 1906, the maple had stood at its old site for fifty-seven years.

Harry Buckley wrote Mrs. Kelly thanking her for the maple:

Your fine cooperation together with the Oregon State Highway Department, Lambert Gardens and the Japanese Garden Society of Oregon, resulted in the moving and planting of this, the first tree to be installed in the new garden. This we hope will be the nucleus of what will become a famous tourist attraction and a source of local pride.

Soon, the city Park Bureau crews under the supervision of William Robinson and following Professor Tono's blueprint, started planting the Flat Garden. Officially, there was no money to pay them. In 1984, Robinson recalled: "I smuggled people in to get this Garden

Aerial view of the nascent Garden, taken in 1964. The Flat Garden (center), its look akin to a golf course sand trap, has been leveled, laid out, with many plants in place.
The dry gunnite pond and joining stream beds wander at the bottom. The Sand and Stone Garden's walls, stones and sand are in place (upper center).

(Portland City Archives)

HUMAN NATURE

This ground-level view (again taken in 1964) shows the wire-supported gunnite bed
of the upper pond, and the stream descending toward the lower pond.
Some stones are in place, but the Moon Bridge and planting have not started.
Compare with view on page 24.

(Portland City Archives)

DEDICATION TO GROWTH: A SHORT HISTORY   101

started, sending in crews on weekends because there wasn't any tax money to support it."

The Garden Society was already working with a list of plants sent from Tokyo by Professor Tono. They sent him a list of plants that were approved for shipping to the United States from Japan, letting him know that plants from abroad always had to be quarantined. With the help of Mayor Schrunk, azaleas and rhododendrons (250 red, and 50 white seedlings) were donated by the Tokyo Metropolitan Government. They arrived and were quarantined in Seattle on 22 January 1963, but due to United States Customs-ordered fumigation by the USDA, only about one-sixth of them survived.

As work progressed, the striking weeping cherry (*Prunus subhirtella* 'Pendula') that holds sway over the south side of the Flat Garden was donated—recycled—by Dr. and Mrs. George Y. Marumoto. Another of the countless examples of re-using extant plants and other materials, the tree was saved from a project to widen NE San Rafael Street. As the sole weeping cherry in the Garden— Tono felt that these trees can detract from other plants—it balances the sand area with the Flat Garden's striking maple. About the same time, several Japanese dogwood trees were purchased for the Garden.

During this period, Professor Tono made two quick visits to Portland. Harry Buckley wrote the designer two weeks before the latter's late-November arrival in Portland: "It is expected that all of the major stones for the 'Flat Garden' will be at the garden site by November 20 . . . . We hope to have 50 tons available for your selection and placement."

Tono supervised the detailing of the Flat Garden, putting in place, on four extraordinarily wet days in November 1963, the stone bridge that anchors the southwestern portion of the area, the first stone construction on the site. The stones for this bridge (brought in by the Portland Park Bureau) came from a rock quarry in the Bear Springs area near Mt. Hood. It is amidst some of the azaleas donated that year by the City of Tokyo.

About the same time, the Society began to receive gifts of stone works that today grace the Garden. Six weeks before the formal contract with the Garden was signed on 23 December, the Society received a major gift of the Sapporo Pagoda Lantern, which today acts as the axis around which the whole Garden symbolically revolves. The donors were: The Sapporo Sister City Affiliation Committee, Sapporo Chamber of Commerce, Sapporo Jr. Chamber of Commerce, East Sapporo Rotary Club, Central Lions Club, and City of Sapporo.

On 11 November 1963, on the occasion of Mayor Schrunk's visit to Sapporo, that city's mayor, Yosaku Harada, presented the magnificent five-tiered Sapporo Pagoda to the Japanese Garden. Mayor Harada's letter of transmittal to Mayor Schrunk stated:

> I sincerely hope that this elaborate product modeled after a pagoda will be set in the Japanese Garden which, I am glad to hear, is being constructed in your City of Portland and that this gift from your sister city will remain for long as a token of our good will and everlasting friendship toward our sister city in the United States.

The hand-carved, eighteen-foot pagoda had been located for years at Mr. Shoichi Sugawara's Hokkaido mansion.

The city needed some help from the United States Foreign Service to get the lantern on the ss *Idaho*. The sixty-year-old piece was shipped to Portland in thirteen crates. The two-ton structure, made from Shikoku Island granite, left Otaru on 9 December, arriving on the Willamette on the 27th of the month. It was accepted by city resolution on 3 February 1964, and on the 13th of May there was an official transfer. Since it would take some time to prepare the concrete base for this heavy structure, the Sapporo Pagoda Lantern was loaned to the Art Museum from 16 to 29 March.

Concern for the valuable plants and artifacts placed in the Garden created a need for security that was met locally by Schnitzer Steel Products of Portland. Working with the City of Tokyo (and its mayor Ryotaro Azuma), Morris Schnitzer's firm shipped chain-link steel fencing donated by the Japan Iron and Steel Exporters' Association. This first security fence was placed around the Garden in 1964. (A second, and more complete and secure, fence was put in place in 1985. Again, the Japan Iron and Steel Exporters' Association donated the materials in response to a request from Mildred Schnitzer, through Schnitzer Steel.)

The Harp Lantern (*kotoji doro*) now beautifully integrated into the stream area between the two Strolling Ponds, was donated by the mayor of the old castle city of Kanazawa on the Sea of Japan. It matches one in that city's Kenrokuen Garden, considered one of the great landscape gardens of Japan. The lantern, a gift to the City of Roses, arrived from Kyoto (where it was carved) in September 1964, accompanied by these words by the head of Kanazawa's General Affairs Section:

> We believe this lantern will greatly contribute to the betterment of our mutual understanding and friendship as an everlasting bond between our two cities, and hope that your Society will be more active in future for strengthening of amity between our two countries.

Many of the early gifts to the city for the Japanese Garden were acknowledged by resolutions from the city government.

The activities at the Garden, the hard work by city gardeners and volunteers, as well as the continuing generous contributions of plant material, all were increasingly noticed through 1963 and in 1964. In that period, local newspapers, magazines, television and radio stations featured the Garden on more than eighty occasions.

Although the enormous project—strapped for cash and depending on volunteers and donations—was moving ahead, the Society was under pressure to meet deadlines, to get the job done. The first years were filled with "footwork, phoning and planning," according to long-time Board member Mildred Schnitzer. On 7 August 1964, "an emergency" was declared by a city ordinance so that work could move ahead on the Garden. This action made it possible for a five-year lease agreement between the city and the Garden to be signed, for the Society's use of the city's property. (The lease has been reviewed and renewed every five years since then.) The city's deep contribution to the early Garden continued, and during 1964–65, excavating, clearing, landscaping, irrigation, plumbing work and planting was done officially through the agency of the Portland Park Bureau. Their participation enabled crews to build the Heavenly Falls, one of the major construction projects of 1964–65. Heavy machinery was used to remove or relocate tons of old zoo stone. and to bring in new stones specially selected for the Heavenly Falls. Hundreds of tons of soil were trucked through Washington Park to give shape and contour to the backdrop hill behind the lower pond.

By 12 November 1964, the Society was able to sponsor a special members-only open house tour of the Garden. Professor Tono attended to begin introducing—to a positive response—the Society supporters to what the Garden was going to become.

Due to the progress in the Garden, gifts (in money, materials and plants) increased substantially. In April, the Society estimated the total cost of the Garden would be nearly $450,000, and projected that the Garden would be done by late 1967. By the end of 1965, much of the form of the Garden, as a visitor sees it today, was completed. Such basics as a buried electrical system and pumps for the waterfalls were in place. Ponds and watercourses had been constructed, the trail through the Garden had been graded, and the zoo's remnant rest rooms were upgraded.

By August, the Flat Garden, with the gourd and saucer mounds and the temporary gravel in place, was eighty-percent complete; the Sand and Stone Garden, with its walls up, but without their tile cap, was seventy-five-percent finished.

One of the Garden's striking structures, the Wisteria Arbor, was built in 1965. The supporting arbor, made of concrete to simulate bark-covered wood, was originally planned to be made of bamboo and redwood. However, both Portland's wet winters and the eventual weight of the wisteria obviated against such a flimsy structure. Part of the cost of the arbor was defrayed by a gift from Eastmoreland Garden Club members in memory of Lt. Roger Okamoto, who lost his life in Vietnam. The Chinese wisteria was donated by 7-DS Nursery of Portland.

For four years, the Society had been planting and building the Garden. The public was as curious as one newspaper noted, that "progress [on the Garden] has been as mysterious as the Orient itself." With all that had been accomplished to date, the Board felt that the time was right to open the Garden for a free public viewing. On 13 September 1965, the gates opened, the pumps for the Strolling Pond Garden's two waterfalls were "activated," and Portlanders had their first—and week-long—look at the Garden. The Society's move proved to be a great success. Nearly ten thousand persons—six thousand of them on a weekend alone—took their first enthusiastic walk through the rough beginnings of Portland's great Garden. Two months later, in November, Mayor Schrunk proudly led an official delegation from Sapporo through the Garden.

Under the guidance of Garden President Thaddeus Bruno, a Women's Council (which came to be known as the Activities Council) was formed in 1965. Bruno stated that the "purpose of the council will be to carry out the social, educational and cultural program of the Japanese Garden Society," sponsoring events that supported the purposes of the Garden. The Council's first occasion introduced Governor Mark Hatfield to all the architectural renderings and plans for the Garden in a September event attended by over three hundred women at the Portland Garden Club.

The re-use of mature plant materials from around the Portland metropolitan area continued in 1965. Eight large Japanese black pines were saved from destruction during the construction of a parking garage at the University of Oregon Medical School (now OHSU). These gifts to the park department were removed and replanted by cranes; they were transported on trucks to the Garden. (The city agreed to "trade" other types of trees from its nursery stock for these pines.) A fine maple tree that now stands near the Stone Bridge in the Flat Garden was removed from Water Bureau property at Dodge Park on the Sandy River. Much that is necessary for the smooth operation of the Garden is hidden; in 1965, the underground electric lines were in under the Flat Garden.

In 1966 and 1967, several finishing touches were added to the Garden. The Flat Garden, all the waterfalls throughout the Strolling Pond Garden, and the Sand Garden were nearly finished. The Garden's centerpiece, the original Moon Bridge, donated by the Truman Collins Foundation, was completed by the George Moore Co. (A request for bids on installing an aggregate walk from the

The City or Portland provided workers and equipment to bring into reality Professor Tono's vision of the Japanese Garden. In this mid-1960's photograph, the machine in the middle is placing heavy stones at the base of the Moon Bridge. For a decade the city provided equipment to the Garden.

(William Robinson photograph)

Wisteria Arbor to the Moon Bridge into Strolling Pond Garden and down into the Natural Garden were sent out in 1968. This contract was never let, and much of the area remains graveled to this day.)

In May 1966, Tono arrived once more in Portland for a five-week stay. During that time he was to complete the final planning of the Garden. He supervised the placement of major stones and trees and much of the shrubbery. With great care he placed the stone lanterns and basins that the Garden had in its possession at that time, as well as the bronze cranes at the west side of the upper pond. The placement of stones in the various watercourses was yet to be done. Tono also selected flowering cherries, the cost of which was underwritten by First National Bank of Oregon as part of that bank's centennial. He also chose where the trees would be planted. Planting took place that fall with Garden President Thaddeus Bruno and bank president Ralph J. Voss helping place the first Kwanzan cherry.

In 1966, the Portland Garden Club donated substantial funds to underwrite the creation of the two iris gardens. Located on both sides of the main stream between the upper and lower ponds, and just below the Shrine Waterfall, these gardens were stocked with plants from the Marx Gardens of Boring and the Cooley Gardens of Silverton. The bulbs were in place by spring of 1967, and flowered with their first blooms that June. (Every few years the iris rhizomes are separated, which can often hinder their blooming for that year.) About this time the city aided by placing in the Garden a long-over-due alarm system.

In July and August 1966, for the first time since the previous September, the Garden opened its gates to the public on weekends, drawing about a thousand persons a day. In 1967, when the Garden opened briefly for seven days in May; 29,000 paid the nominal

HUMAN NATURE

admission fee and passed through the gate. The *Oregonian* referred to a visit to the Garden as "serenity for sale: 50 cents." These were the Garden's first steps toward becoming an all-year attraction.

In 1968, Society President Bill deWeese and others became enamored of the greenish Iyo stones while visiting the Inland Sea island of Shikoku. At deWeese's request Professor Tono selected a special, tall Shikoku Iyo stone, with two small companion stones. They now stand at the southwest corner of the Pavilion, in honor of the Society's first president, Philip Englehart, who died during the year. Englehart was remembered at that time as a man with "a very searching mind . . . [who had] visions beyond his own time."

In 1969, during another visit, Professor Tono planted the north hillside above the upper Strolling Pond Garden with Rhododendron 'Mucronatum' (*Azalea indica alba*), as a living memorial to Englehart, who loved these white flowering shrubs.

Later that year, deWeese finalized the purchase of sacks of Kyoto-area Shirakawa River white granite sand. This was used to replace the original (and inappropriate) sand in the Flat Garden and the Sand and Stone Garden. Over twelve-hundred 100-pound bags of the sand finally arrived, shipped courtesy of deWeese's Esco Corp.

In 1968, plans were well on the way for two major structures to be added to the Garden: the Entry Gate and the Tea House. The Entry Gate would be built on site, and the Tea House would be built in Japan, taken apart and re-assembled in Portland. President Thaddeus Bruno knew that "you cannot build a thing such as this rattling a tin cup." Bruno convinced Howard Vollum, president of Tektronix, to have both Tektronix and Sony Tek commit to supporting the costs of the Tea House. Bruno said to Vollum: "It would mean more to what we are trying to do with this garden in the way of promoting a

Japanese-Portland relationship in trade and goodwill if Sony Tek would do it than if would if we had some anonymous donation. . . . I would like Sony Tek . . . to build that tea house for us."

The Tea House was built by Japan's Kajima Construction Co., a company that builds large, modern structures, but is also known for its work in producing traditional buildings. Today the Tea House sits in its own garden, much of which was underwritten by the U.S. National Bank of Oregon.

With Mayor Schrunk in attendance, the Tea House and the Iyo stone were dedicated in a rainstorm on 1 June 1968. Tea Master Soi Yamada, who headed the Sohen-ruiji School in Kamakura, performed the dedication tea ceremony. Later that year, the Poetry Stone, that stands now at the Sand and Stone Garden overlook, arrived as a gift from the Tokyo Stone Co.

It was becoming clear that the Japanese Garden was going to be a success. Growing public interest, as well as volunteer, Board and corporate support seemed to assure this. The Garden had clearly fledged, and some perceived a need for forging new relationships. On 17 June 1968, Roland B. Hall, director of operations for the Bureau of Parks, wrote to Superintendent Harry Buckley:

> Since the origin of the Japanese Garden authorized by Ordinance No. 117188 dated August 7, 1963, wherein the city of Portland was to have provided technical assistance to the Garden Society, the Bureau of Parks has provided the services, equipment, plant materials and manpower to construct a major portion of this garden using funds for general park maintenance. . . . [A]ny further additions to the Japanese Garden become the responsibility of the Japanese Garden Society and that all further improvement cost be defrayed from donations and admission charges.

As a result of this memo, the City of Portland and the Garden Society concluded another formal agreement authorizing the city and the Japanese Garden Society of Oregon to maintain "a formal Japanese garden on Park Bureau property."

From correspondence addressed to members of the city government, it was clear that the Garden was becoming a place of great value to Portland leaders. Clarence W. Walls, of the Men's Garden Club of Portland, who had toured the Garden the previous weekend, sent a letter to City Commissioner Frank Ivancie on 7 August 1968:

> I had never really appreciated the work 'over and beyond the call of duty' which the men of our Park Department have put, and are continuing to put, into this wonderful project. They have spent their own time and gasoline on week-ends hunting for the right rocks to create the picture Professor Tono is creating for us and for posterity . . . . But without the untiring work of these men of the Park Bureau, the dream could not have been reality.

In 1968, Hoichi Kurisu arrived as the second on-site landscape director from Japan (succeeding Kinya Hira). As would the directors who came after him, Kurisu began to leave his own imprint on the Garden. He felt his two main purposes were to "express Professor Tono's controlling design, according to his wishes and sketches," and to "make the Garden mature" by concentrating on "detail work." To do that meant that the gardeners had to control the new shoots, to avoid at all costs a "neglected feeling," and to control and trim the pines. Kurisu was concerned about how green were the lawns, and leaned toward making them "accents" in the Garden.

In the 1970s, after less than a decade, the Garden began to come of age. People in Portland began to respond to the Garden's presence.

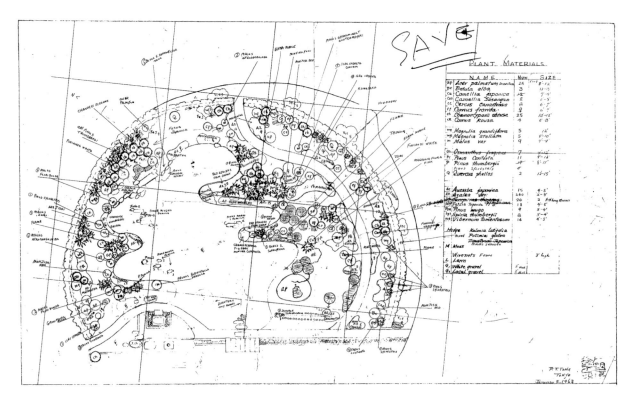

The number of plants introduced to the old Washington Park Zoo site is staggering.
Illustrated here is a planting scheme signed off by Professor Tono in January 1963.
Even if all these plants may have been placed exactly as marked,
constant compositional adjustment and replacement over time
means that today's plant-by-plant organization can be radically different.
Yet the Garden's general layout remains dedicated to Professor Tono's vision.

(Portland City Archives)

Problems with original design details or plants had to be dealt with, and financial difficulties had to be faced and surmounted.

In 1970, a nurseryman from Milwaukie, Oregon, E.T. Watanabe, donated a large seventy-five-year-old coast pine (*Pinus contorta*) to the Garden. It has suffered—with trunk-bending resilience—through ice storms and has been moved, but it remains a sentinel at the Entry Gate.

Professor Tono designed and built a stone "mountain" near the Sapporo Pagoda Lantern in 1970. Some time later, one of the gardeners inadvertently moved the stones into the Natural Garden, and it was never rebuilt.

Also, as it entered a new decade, the Garden held its first *bonsai* exhibition; the planters were arranged in the area below the Moon Bridge. Since that time, *bonsai* shows have become a staple of the Garden's annual activities schedule; today, the shows take place in the more convenient Pavilion.

Not everything at the Garden was popular with the public, however. In 1971, in answer to some correspondence about the lower gate cutting off joggers from "the extensive system of hiking and jogging trails throughout the park and the arboretum," the Garden set in motion a plan that eventually opened up the fence adjacent to the gate. (To this day, runners have access to the running trails, via the access road; the Garden itself is off limits during closed hours.)

In 1972, Rowena Newton became the Garden's executive secretary, succeeding the original secretary, Ruby Hildebrand. (For years Newton referred to her office in the old zoo rest-room building as the "Flushing Castle.") A month after Newton took on her new post, the Society's first "newsletter" was issued; it was later named *The Garden Path*.

This was also a year of surprises, completions and gifts. An unexpected anonymous gift of $100,000, made in the memory of Mr. and Mrs. Thomas Hall, helped the Society's finances. In 1972, Rod Johnson, of radio station KWJJ, donated the Japanese red pine that stands protectively over the benches just outside the Entry Gate.

The April issue of *Sunset* magazine featured the Garden; in the summer the volunteer guide program was instituted (a major upgrade of the program would take place in 1978); by the end of the year, the wall at the north end of the Strolling Pond Garden along with the wooden service gate were completed.

However, it was not all positive news in 1972. The gardeners were forced to replace the cut-leaf maple that had been donated for the Flat Garden in 1963. Planted at the surface level, its roots had rotted and this wonderful tree had died. It was replaced by another cut-leaf maple donated by Mrs. Robert Brown of Portland's Sellwood district. This one was planted above the surface of the Flat Garden with the earth built up around it, a suggestion for "growing healthy maples" made by Tono. At the same time, a large Akebono cherry (*Prunus x yedoensis* 'Akebono') was moved to its present location on Cherry Hill behind the Sapporo Pagoda. It was originally donated in 1963 by Mrs. Sam Panzica because of a street-widening project.

In 1973, the Society negotiated a renewal of its lease with the city. But they also negotiated the addition of nearly five acres of land north of the Garden that contains the entrance road, the parking area on Kingston Street, and other land surrounding the Garden was added to the lease to protect the Garden's location from development by residential builders. This change also protected the "environmental zone" in keeping with the city's master plan. With the addition of the undeveloped hillside, the access road and its verges, the area up to Wildwood Trail and land contiguous to Kingston Avenue, the

Garden's jurisdiction now stands at about ten acres. The City of Portland continues to lease this acreage to the Japanese Garden for one dollar a year, as it has since 1963.

In 1973, more additions were made to the Garden. Another large stone from Shikoku island was donated by the Japanese government and placed near the large maple in the Flat Garden. A maple, grown from the seed from the Emperor's garden in Japan, was donated by Mrs. Edmund Hayes. Mrs. Mark Sumida donated forty-one koi (Japanese carp) for the Strolling Pond Garden. They would die from chlorine poisoning used in cleaning the ponds in 1974; Mrs. Sumida generously donated more fish. Today, cleaning of the pools requires enormous care to protect the koi, and provides one of the most fascinating occurrences in the Garden, as gardeners and entrance staff run the fish, one at a time from the pool to be cleaned to the other water area in the Strolling Pond Garden. Koi are also subject to depredation from raccoons, who gain entrance into the Garden at night, and are fond of angling for these beautiful and valuable fish.

As attendance grew, amenities for visitors became a necessity. Made out of one cedar tree from the nearby woods, a number of new Tono-designed benches were placed around the Garden. They were built by Garden employee, Ben Muzzell. New ones (with memorial plaques) were produced in 1995.

In the original agreement between the Japanese Garden Society and the City of Portland, the Society had agreed to reimburse the city for all expenses for the Garden accumulated by the municipality, beyond the nominal annual lease payment. In 1974, Board President William deWeese realistically told the city that the Society could not meet that obligation; the Society already had to default on its bank loans. The city agreed to cancel the Garden's obligation, and remove

Flat Garden in 1974, six years before the Pavilion was built.
In Takuma Tono's mind, this area would not be fully realized until there was a raised view of it, as is now afforded from the west verandah.
The edge of that porch area sits on the line of the low fence pictured here.
The original plantings of the saucer and the gourd were deemed inappropriate.
The pink ruby dianthus (shown here) was later changed to woolly thyme.

(William Robinson photograph)

all of its support, save one gardener, in the future. The city has, in fact, carried the sizable cost of water over the years.

Andy Rocchia, long-time garden writer with the Portland *Oregonian*, purchased for the Garden a boxwood tree (*Buxus semper-virens* 'Arborescens') that had stood for years on the old grounds of St. Mary's Academy—a downtown Portland Roman Catholic school for girls. A new school had been constructed across the street from the old and unsafe original building. In the interim, in 1975, at the sw Fourth and Market site of St. Mary's, the boxwood was hung with a sign: "Please don't cut me down. I may be going to the Japanese Garden Society and can't be moved till Sept. 15. Thank you." The box-wood now stands across the graveled path from the western end of the Moon Bridge.

Not all plants survive transplantation—or planting—in the Japanese Garden. An effort to grow lotus plants from roots produced from seeds over two thousand years old failed; they appeared to find the climate in Oregon too cold.

Vandalism has proven a problem during the Garden's history. In 1975, over $3,000 worth of damage was done; one of the first lanterns donated to the Garden, was stolen within two weeks of its placement. This was a wooden post lantern, a traditional form for lighting ancient roadways, which had arrived in June 1964 as a gift from the Tokyo Yacht Works. During one night in the late 1980s vandals attacked areas throughout the Garden. They damaged the Antique Gate, and in the Strolling Pond Garden, fences and the Zigzag Bridge railings were destroyed, and the heavy wooden benches were cast into the upper pond. Among other acts of civil cowardice, the guardian lions had been dumped on their sides. The lions and many of the lanterns have been toppled a number of times.

The Board agreed to build a pavilion on the site chosen by Professor Tono more than a decade earlier, just east of the sand portion of the Flat Garden. Garden President Rudie Wilhelm noted, "If we can't raise money for this, there is something wrong with us." The city allocated up to $50,000 on the $500,000 Pavilion in 1979, under a special appropriation unit. The World Exposition Commemorative Fund of Japan pledged $100,000 to the Pavilion fund. The large metal flag pole now east of the Pavilion on the city side was donated by Pacific Metal Co.

Architect David Pugh, of Skidmore, Owings and Merrill, was asked to go ahead with plans for the Pavilion, and by the end of the year a quarter of the $550,000 needed was in hand. Forty-foot holes had to be dug to test the earth and support for the forthcoming Pavilion.

Ground was broken for the Garden's great building on 17 August. By December most of the money had been raised, helped by a contribution from Portland's sister city, Sapporo, of ¥150,000.

The Garden's largest, and signature, building's opening was accompanied by a once-in-a-lifetime event. Just as the ceremony took place at 3:00 PM on 18 March 1980, Mt. St. Helens erupted. A woman in attendance said: "Just like Japan, a volcano erupts for a special occasion." The moneys raised paid for the Pavilion, the aggregate walkway from the entrance, around both sides of the Flat Garden, and helped start an endowment fund.

Activities remained keen in 1977, as plantings and rocks replaced an old "construction driveway" just to the left of the Chinese Wisteria Gate. A white dogwood was purchased with funds established in honor of Professor Elizabeth Drews, and a Japanese persimmon tree was donated. Mr. and Mrs. Mark Sumida donated nearly $5,000 worth of additional carp. Dr. James Frohnmayer donated a seventy-five-year-old lace-leaf maple. In 1977–78, Garden membership neared 1,000 for the first time.

The prime minister of Japan, Takao Fukuda, visited in 1978, and "was impressed with the size and beauty of the Garden." He added: "Portland's Japanese Garden is the most authentic I have seen outside of Japan." It probably was hard for the Japanese leader to really enjoy the Garden, because, commented Newton, Fukuda, he was "in the center of a beehive" of security personnel, politicians and reporters. Prior to his visit, Federal agents had dogs sniff the whole site.

It was easier to bring the prime minister to the Garden than plants from his homeland. Plant material coming into the United States remains a problem, and some timber bamboo brought in from Japan the same year, had to be steam-treated to decontaminate it.

In 1979, the Olympic Lantern in the Flat Garden was donated by Dr. and Mrs. Walter Lobitz. That year Tri-Met, which operates the Portland area bus and light rail services, started the No. 63 bus service to the Garden, Metro Zoo and the Oregon Museum of Science and Industry (OMSI) then located in Washington Park. This brought much-needed direct and scheduled service to the site.

Many visitors cannot negotiate the pathway from the Kingston parking lot to the Entry Gate, so a free shuttle service was a priority. Over time, this has proved popular, and having a vehicle in service during the summer months has been a constant (and an expensive) service provided by the Society. Replacing a vehicle near death, the second shuttle bus was purchased in 1980; it was acquired for the dedication of the Pavilion. In the 1990s, the two handicapped parking slots were designated in the upper employee lot.

More and more associations with the Garden have been created over time, and one of these, the Kashin Tei Kai, was formed in 1980 to care for the Tea House and the utensils used in the tea ceremony.

After a decade of staunch service, Rowena Newton resigned in 1981 when she moved out of the state. Patricia Morrison, a person with "immense horticultural knowledge," took her place on 1 May.

For years, the Garden was closed during the winter, opening on 1 April for summer, to be closed again at the end of October. However, in the fall of 1981, William Robinson suggested that the Garden should remain open throughout the winter. While there were some doubters, Robinson proved prescient; after a month-long trial period, during which he personally manned the gate, it became obvious that the winter hours were a success. Since that time the Garden has remained open except for Thanksgiving, Christmas and New Year's Day.

On 24 May 1985, William Robinson was awarded the Order of the Sacred Treasure, Sixth Class, by Japanese Emperor Hirohito. The ceremony was held at Consul General Kunio Kamoshida's home in Portland. Robinson received the award for helping foster "civilization, friendship and peace" through the Japanese Garden. (Four other persons—former Society presidents William deWeese, Rudie Wilhelm and Cliff Alterman, as well as long-time Society Board member Mildred Schnitzer—have received awards from the Japanese emperor for efforts related to Japanese-American relations well beyond the confines of the Garden.)

For over twenty years, the persons working on the Garden's landscape had inadequate work, storage and changing facilities. The old zoo's "meat house," which had been the storage area for the caged animals' food, had barely served the gardeners' needs. In 1985, the $375,000 Alaskan cedar Garden House (*tsumesho*) was completed. Designed by Skidmore, Owings and Merrill as a "typical Japanese building" it was dedicated by a Shinto priest. Its traditional lines add a new authentic element to the Garden's landscape, while it houses gardening equipment, showers and a staff locker room, as well as parking space for the shuttle-bus, Cushman, and a pickup.

The same year found the Waterscapes area of the lower Natural Garden put in place—a $35,000 project.

As the American scene has evolved over the past four decades, the view of Board members has changed, reflecting the changes in society. The early Board members were inspired by Professor's Tono's vision, and, according to Schnitzer, it had to be "ethically correct . . . it has to be *shibui*." "We held on to the tradition." Today, as with all non-profits, the Japanese Garden Society must face the Board scrutiny of the "bottom line" while maintaining a commitment to the original purposes of the Garden, which were "to establish, maintain, improve, operate and administer a formal Japanese Garden in the City of Portland, Oregon, for educational, scientific, cultural, literary and charitable purposes."

The Garden's designer, and long-time patron, Professor Tono died in 1987 at the age of 96.

In November of that year, Maureen Yandle Sanchez was hired as the Garden's activities coordinator. Her responsibility was to plan and execute the Garden's 1988 twenty-fifth anniversary celebration. However, so skilled was her coordination of this event, she was made acting executive director in 1989. Later that year, the Board approved a full-time executive director position. Sanchez was offered the job, and officially assumed the position on 1 January 1990.

By 1988, the Society membership had grown to 3,200. Reflecting how the Garden is used, and its broad generational appeal, most of the memberships fell within the family category. From 1979 to 1988 gate receipts climbed from $96,432 to $293,628. The total income from all sources during the later year was $460,000, which was a remarkable growth of three-hundred percent over the same period.

William deWeese's Hillside Garden was formally dedicated on 5 November 1989. The stones in the Hillside Garden itself were from deWeese's home (as were all the plantings); those stones around the base of the hill at the paved drive, are from Ripplebrook, Oregon.

In August of the silver anniversary year, Nobuo Matsunaga, Ambassador to the United States from Japan, visited the Garden. During his stay, at a luncheon attended by both Governor Neil Goldschmidt and Senator Mark Hatfield, Matsunaga described the Japanese Garden as "the most beautiful Japanese garden, not only in the United States, but in the whole world outside of Japan." It is an appellation that the Garden has guarded through vigilant maintenance and planning ever since. Adding to the Garden's silver celebration, Portland mayor, J.E. "Bud" Clark, declared 1989 "The Year of the Portland Japanese Garden." Twenty-five new cherry trees, in memory of Dr. Robert Dodge, were planted in 1989 on either side of the Entry Gate.

Some forty-year-old trees were recycled to the Garden due to construction at the Oregon Health Sciences Dental School complex. Four of the maples (saved by long-time Garden Board member and supporter, School of Dentistry professor Dr. Hiroshi Ueno) stand on the walkway between the Entry Gate and the Pavilion.

To deal with the ongoing problem of vandalism, the Board approved construction of an additional security fence along the north side of the Garden area, including the deWeese Hillside and upper parking area gate. There were additional concerns about security for the Garden, and money was raised to add walls to the Antique Gate, a new chain-link fence along the north side of the Garden property, and another steel gate across the access road near the Hillside Garden.

Long-range planning for the Garden got under way in 1989, and the resultant publication, *The Garden Way: The Plan of the Japanese Garden Society of Oregon*, was issued in November 1990. This plan detailed the first quarter-century's many accomplishments. It was designed to aid all involved with running the Garden by providing a framework for the near future. One of the strengths of the Garden, according to this study, has been the notable volunteer contributions that have brought about so much success; its estimated that volunteers had by that time given over one million hours of labor, guidance, and enthusiasm.

As with so many aspects of life, the strength of the Garden's striking location is also its potential weakness. A minor earthquake in 1989 jolted the site and damaged ponds in the Natural Garden. As a result, Board members discovered that the whole Garden is built on an old landslide. The wonderful swale that forms the western edge of the site, and gives interest and diversity to the area's topography, is the result of a large flow of soil from a "headscarp" on the hillside above. This flow produces a "crown" of debris on which now rests the Flat Garden and the Pavilion. The Garden is in what a soil engineer called a "sub-sag" area of the slide.

Concern about the stability of the whole hillside, prompted the Executive Committee to request a report from a technical expert. That report stated that the area had been undergoing subsidence since 1894—and predicted that the hill would continue to creep at a rate of up to one inch a year. As a result of this slippage, the Garden was faced with substantial leakage in the large pond in the Natural Garden, which eventually lead to major repairs in 1990, at a cost of $10,000.

Today, the Garden staff constantly monitors the movement of the ten acres that it oversees. Day-to-day there are few concerns; over the lifetime of the Garden there will be continuous need to review and repair to keep the site secure.

Late in 1989, the city's three-year program of pruning limbs that had blocked portions of the borrowed scenery view east across Portland to the Cascades and the Columbia River Gorge—was completed without the removal of a single tree. The Cascade peaks of Rainier, St. Helens, Adams and Hood can now be seen from the Pavilion's east verandah.

In 1990, an increasing social use of the Garden was much in evidence. The "Second Sunday Series" of lectures and other Garden-related events started. The International Rotary Convention in Portland in June produced the single-day attendance record, when over two thousand conventioneers—nearly ten times the average daily attendance—swarmed over the Garden.

In an effort to give broader representation on the Board to interested co-organizations the bylaws were changed, in 1990, to include a representative of the important Japanese businessmen's organization, Shokookai of Oregon.

The Garden always has been a favorite of the media. Numerous television stations have featured it on screen, and hundreds of articles have appeared in the *Oregonian*, and in other general circulation journals. In 1991, alone, for example, issues of *House Beautiful*, *House and Garden*, and *Elle Decor*, all ran stories on the Garden.

As a result of the soil consultant's report, landscape director Tohru Tanaka's bold plan for the Hirsch Viewpoint Garden had to be tabled. (The Garden was to be in memory of Harold Hirsch, the Garden's first long-range planning chairman.) Tanaka had envisioned, among other things, a substantial stone wall that would echo (on a smaller scale) the massive walls surrounding Japanese feudal castles. The weight, however, would have proved a burden on such a

In 1994 the Japanese Garden's
new Service Center was completed.
Replacing the last building left over
from the old Portland Zoo,
this building houses
public rest rooms, storage areas
and the Gift Shop.
This view of the building
is from inside the Entry Gate.

(Allan Mandell photograph)

fragile site. Masayuki Mizuno was charged with coming up with a design that would be appropriate in appearance and would stabilize the soil. By 1992 Mizuno had completed the master plan for the Hirsch Viewpoint Garden and installed the bamboo fencing he had designed.

On 22 August 1991, thirty-one tea masters from Japan performed the tea ceremony for the public in the Garden's Pavilion. Two months later, the large, white-barked birch trees that had grown to inappropriately dominate the Flat Garden were cut down and removed

Also in 1991, the new Tea House viewing area off the upper pond was completed. The fall of 1992 the Kashin Tei Kai tea group presented the Garden a black lacquer tea ceremony table—a *misono dana*—a gift from Japan's Toyama Prefecture.

The Board agreed, in June 1992, on a design for the long-needed Service Center. This building would replace the antiquated zoo rest room building that at one time housed the "swamp," as the staff called the tiny pre-Pavilion administrative offices. The new facility would house the Gift Shop, rest rooms that met Americans with Disabilities Act (ADA) regulations, and a large storage area in its basement. While there were some concerns about the "tone" the presence of a retail outlet would establish, there was little disagreement over the need to have some kind of retail outlet to satisfy constant requests from Garden visitors. The Service Center required a major upgrade of the outdated sewer system. However, the upgrade would alleviate some trying problems the Garden staff was having with the pumping of water for the Strolling Pond.

Ground was broken for the Service Center in September 1993; the decades-old zoo rest room building was demolished in December, and R & H Construction began the real building work. Designed by area architect Richard McBride of McBride Architects (who had participated in the design process of the Pavilion), the Service Center was the first building at the Garden constructed to meet ADA specifications. A coin representing longevity and patience was placed in one of the column forms before concrete was poured. Early in 1994, a set of large stones was placed between the Service Center and the upper pond as part of the re-landscaping project brought on by the new building. On 28 May 1994, with special Shinto ceremonies, the Service Center and its Gift Shop were blessed and opened to the public.

Revenue generated from all sources in 1993 reached a new high, $818,000, the last year before substantial infusion of additional support would be provided by the Gift Shop.

It was decided for safety reasons to close the Bill deWeese Hillside Garden in 1993. In a litigious America, its steep pathways, and uncertain footing loomed too dangerously for the Garden to take any chances. The Hillside Garden has been maintained since that time as a lovely backdrop as the visitor enters the Garden, but not as a formal garden itself.

In mid-1994, the Garden Board re-awakened the idea of providing a tram from the public parking area up to the Entry Gate. This was not a new idea; Professor Tono had shown a conveyance of some kind in his early renderings of the Garden. The Board faced the constant complaint about the difficulty for many Garden visitors to climb the steep hill to the Entry Gate. A fiscal reason for considering the tramway arose from the surprisingly high cost of maintaining the shuttle-bus service each summer; insurance and maintenance costs continue to be nearly prohibitive.

After thirty years—one-hundred-and-twenty seasons—of changing weather, at least five hundred rakings of new patterns, the accumulation of city grime, and simple aging, the white sand in the

Sand and Stone Garden had darkened and deteriorated considerably, by 1994. Under the direction of garden consultant Masayuki Mizuno, the gardeners re-set the stones in this area, adding areas for moss around the base of each. The old sand in this severe garden was removed and replaced with new, and brighter Kyoto-area Shirakawa River sands. The Garden's little Cushman cart moved over forty cubic yards of new sand down to the Sand and Stone Garden, and as much again back up a non-public pathway to the Flat Garden.

Following the Garden's long tradition of recycling, the gardeners washed the old sand and mixed and melded it with the extant Shirakawa sand already in the Flat Garden. The addition of this restored material afforded the gardeners a deeper layer for better and more pronounced raking patterns in the Flat Garden.

Thousands of persons (from the Board, through the members and volunteers) have held the Garden close to their hearts. However, day-to-day, its the intimate care of the Garden's roster of careful gardeners that has made, in the long run, the greatest difference to the look and quality of the place. Especially important have been the landscape directors from Japan in first twenty-five years: Kinya Hira, Hoichi Kurisu, Hachiro Sakakibara, Michio Wakui, Masayuki Mizuno, Kichiro Sano, Takao Donuma, Tohru Tanaka.

By 1965, and to follow the lead given by the Garden's designer, Professor Takuma Tono, it was becoming clear to the Garden Society that bringing in new gardeners trained in the tradition in Japan for three-year stints was going to become a necessity. Those gardeners have carried on the continuity of Tono's vision, and provided the training for those now charged with maintaining the Garden.

However, it was not until 1968 that the first of the gardener's trailer houses was stationed just outside the Garden near the Entry Gate; later, a second trailer was placed on the hill above the Tea House. Kinya Hira was the first Japanese gardener brought in to work in the Garden. Hira was brought to the Garden by Professor Tono in 1966 for a three-year stint as landscape director. (He left the Garden in 1969 to pursue his own business in Los Angeles.)

Hoichi Kurisu arrived in 1968 to become landscape director. Born near Hiroshima, and a survivor of the atomic attack on that city ("I remember it all—the light, the mushroom cloud."), Kurisu was an American literature major in Japan. He took up gardening "as a balance to the materialism he saw in Los Angeles" where his father had a "landscape maintenance business." He met Professor Tono in the City of Angels, where Tono's daughter lived, but went back to Japan to study under Kenzo Ogata (the designer of the landscaping at Honolulu's East West Center and the Japanese Garden in Seattle).

Kurisu also supervised stone work that made a number of sections of the Garden (e.g. the concrete base of the Moon Bridge) more natural looking. He placed pines above the waterfall in the upper pond garden and finished work on the "natural water basin" near the Entry Gate.

Hachiro Sakakibara ("a tall, slender young fellow") arrived from Japan in 1972. He worked for some time with Kurisu, and then, after Kurisu left to start his own gardening business, finished reworking Tono's Moss Garden, now the Natural Garden. Sakakibara brought a vigorous energy to the maintenance and the detailing of the Garden. Sakakibara returned to Japan in 1973.

William Robinson, as Park Department garden foreman, worked

for ten years from the very beginning on the preparation of the Garden; in 1973 he became the liaison between the Garden and the city, replacing Edward Erickson, Park Department architect. Hugh Shogren, a Park Department gardener, came on site full-time in 1973 and. became full-time Japanese Garden gardener.

Sakakibara's replacement, Michio Wakui, was appointed in December 1973; he arrived at the Garden in January 1974. In his initial year, Wakui began work on the "north hill," outside the Entry Gate, and he built the first suggestion box.

In the outer tea garden, Wakui built the Garden's first *machiai*, in 1975. The shelter, tucked up against the steep western hillside, is designed to provide a place of contemplation before one enters the Tea Garden.

Sharon Riddell, the first woman hired as a gardener, helped Michio Wakui put together the Antique Gate at the lower entrance of the Garden in 1976, but Wakui had to leave the Garden for health reasons late in the year.

Gardeners Michael Giusti (a graduate of Portland Public Schools' "Operation Green Thumb," and now head gardener) first was employed by the Garden in 1975. He and Hugh Shogren cobbled together the misting system from the Moss Garden and made a sprinkling system for the east-side iris beds; they did the same the next year for the west-side ones.

Because of the precipitous departure of Michio Wakui for health reasons in 1976, Hoichi Kurisu stepped in to aid the Garden. He designed the granite pattern for the city overlook section east of the Pavilion.

Masayuki Mizuno, who was born and raised in the Nagoya area, and who received substantial gardening training in Tokyo, arrived in July 1977 to become Garden landscape director. Called "Masa" by his associates, "he was good at maintenance," especially "pruning and wrapping of trees," Rowena Newton said. Mizuno believes it is not good for the Garden to have more than one major project each year. The Garden, according to his beliefs, "has to rest," and the gardeners must simply carefully maintain it.

Under the direct supervision of William Robinson, Youth Conservation Corps members built a trail in the Hillside Garden in 1977 (which is no longer open to the public). On 17 September 1977, Robinson retired from the Park Bureau after thirty years of service, fourteen of which were spent working with the Japanese Garden. In honor of his distinct and unique association, the Garden's Board made him a life member.

Mizuno and the garden staff built the "stone rain trough" in the Moss Garden (it is now just outside the Natural Garden), and added a wall near the bench above that Garden's waterfalls. The stones for this came from the Zigzag area of Mt. Hood National Forest. Mizuno built the three steps at the Entry Gate in 1979.

Just before Masayuki Mizuno left the employ of the Garden, he added sculptured posts to the Zigzag Bridge during the repair of that structure; he also finished the stone work around the Pavilion. He left to start his own Portland-based landscape gardening firm. Hugh Shogren retired in 1980.

Kichiro Sano arrived in 1982 from Japan for a three-year stint as the new landscape director. As with earlier gardeners he lived in the on-site trailer house (now removed) at the edge of the upper parking lot.

Sano's tenure was most activity. Almost at once he repaired and re-landscaped the area around "Saka's Pond" (named for the gardener Hachiro Sakakibara, who built it) in the Natural Garden. He also added the new white sand areas north of the Pavilion.

In 1983, Sano added two small falls to the Strolling Pond Garden stream. It was Sano who erected the first *yuki zuri* in the garden in 1983. Used to protect pine trees from the distorting and breaking weight of winter's ice and snow, these elegant post and rope supports can be seen each winter in the Garden. Sano completed his contracted time and returned to Japan. His replacement Takao Donuma arrived in 1985; he constructed the smal public parking lot garden.

In 1988 former landscape director Hoichi Kurisu, who now had a thriving gardening business based in Portland, was contracted to landscape the upper drive area outside the Entry Gate(with large boulders from near Mt. Hood's Timothy Lake). Kurisu also supervised the planting of the Hillside Garden above the Garden House with plants from William deWeese's home.

Landscape director Donuma, from Niigata, left for his homeland in 1988 before completing his contracted tenure; his father was ill. He did return to do some Japanese fence construction. Tohru Tanaka, was the a landscape director from August 1988 through August 1991.

For the first time in its quarter-century history, in the summer of 1991, the Garden did not have an on-location landscape director native to Japan. With the departure of Tohru Tanaka, who had provided an intense period of change, the job of design and maintenance oversight was now in transition.

Since that time, under the direction of Head Gardener Michael Giusti along with Head Pruner Michael Kondo, the Garden staff has maintained and added to the Garden through its own volition, under guidelines provided by the Garden Committee of the Board, aided by an outside landscape consultant, and former Garden landscape designer, Masayuki Mizuno, the last landscape designer to work in communication with Professor Tono. It is a splendid relationship that continues to this day.

Today, the non-profit corporation (the only non-profit, private Japanese Garden in the United States) is run by a Board of Directors. The Board divides its responsibilities among its executive committee, and additional committees (budget and finance, education, garden, long-range planning, marketing, membership and pavilion use). The Garden is maintained through dues, contributions, gifts, special donations and gate receipts. The Japanese Garden of Portland, Oregon is run without tax support, and is very nearly one hundred percent self supporting. The Garden continues to receive its water from the city and pays Portland an annual lease of one dollar.

It is that rare non-profit organization, one that really pays its own way. As of 1994, membership, gate receipts, and sales in its finely tuned Gift Shop were combined to underwrite well over ninety percent of the Garden's annual operating budget.

It draws more than 120,000 visitors to the Portland area, bringing an infusion to the area's economy that is often overlooked. In addition, the Garden adds to the well-being of the community.

The Japanese Garden has become one of the region's most significant cultural attractions, a place Portlanders and Oregonians in general can bring family and friends to with pride. Through the leadership of its active Board, its superb administrative staff, its set of gardeners with their quiet passion, and its dedicated group of volunteers and members who number in the thousands, it has earned its worldwide reputation. Today, it can be called the finest Japanese garden anywhere in the world outside of Japan. It remains, amidst all its accountable attributes, first and most importantly, a place of relief, restoration and inspiration.

A snow fall emphasizes the touch of human hands in Portland's Japanese Garden.
The Tea House, the sculpted shoreline of the upper pond, the fences,
gates and the Peace Lantern in the foreground—all
part of Human Nature.

(Steve Terrill photograph)

HUMAN NATURE: AN AFTERWORD

A hybrid pieris "Forest Flame" plant surrounds a stone in the Natural Garden.

(Allan Mandell photograph)

Nothing is as it appears. That concept needs to be kept in mind when assessing the meaning of Portland's Japanese Garden. That is not to say that the Garden is anything but beautiful, tranquil, stimulating and, at the same time, edifying; it is to say that this Garden—set as it is nearly 5,000 miles from its host culture—may be part of a process that honors its traditions more than those traditions may be honored at home. This is curious and this is human nature. We watch all traditional cultures, even those traditions that are supposedly the well-spring of our American culture, under siege, daily losing the people who care to nurture the traditions.

The outside view of Japan mistakenly assumes that extreme care is taken to preserve the traditions in, and the historic sites around that island nation. Overuse and the rush of modernization places both that culture and its built manifestations in jeopardy. Japanese school children are required to visit gardens, as they are taught about their traditions. But the insidious, bombarding modern techno-culture tumbles the balance of the culture (as it enters into traditional cultures around the world). This is not new. In a place such as Japan, where borrowing and adapting have been made into an art, this balancing, influencing and adjustment, this radical renewal and change are almost as old as the culture itself.

When the Portland City Council adopted an ordinance creating the Formal Japanese Garden Commission in June 1962, it stated as its goals for the Garden: "This Garden will provide the citizens of Portland with an area of great beauty and serenity and at the same time represent a warm, understandable link with Japan." When surveyed in 1988, the majority of Garden visitors counted "serenity" as their favorite reason for partaking of the Garden.

As former landscape director, Masayuki Mizuno, brings a perspective to what has been done in the mere three decades since Portland's Japanese Gardens was started: "This Garden has progressed much faster than gardens in my homeland. It might have taken fifty years in Japan to do what is done here in five." Adding to the rich success of all who have contributed to make the Garden a success, former president of the Garden's Board, Miles Englehart, states: "This Garden is unique, so well maintained, and so well run. It is a little bit of Japan in the United States."

The Japanese Garden is not merely a place of brilliant spring flowering, though that it is. It is not only an astonishing fall-fired foliage, though that it is. It is not just the soothing softness of fresh snow on every branch, though that it is. It is not simply the dense verdant green of summer, though that it is. The Japanese Garden is all those moments of verity, though it is much more. The Garden is the daily, hourly change, the thousands of nuances, of chance views, of hide and reveal, different for every eye and sense that takes the time to absorb and remember.

A Japanese adage teaches: The garden is not complete until there is no more you can take out of it.

SELECTED SOURCES

Detail of a hydrangea.

(Jerry Stelmack photograph)

All-Japan: The Catalogue of Everything Japanese. Introduction by Oliver Statler. New York: Quil, 1984.

Creating Japanese Gardens. San Ramon, California: Ortho Books, 1989.

Fujioka, Michio. *Japanese Residences and Gardens: A Tradition of Integration.* Translated by H. Mark Horton. Tokyo: Kodansha International, 1982.

The Garden Way: The Plan of the Japanese Garden Society of Oregon. Portland: Japanese Garden Society of Oregon, 1990.

Garratty, John A., and Peter Gay, eds. *The Columbia History of the World.* New York: Harper & Row, 1981.

Itoh, Teiji. *The Gardens of Japan.* Tokyo: Kodansha International, 1984.

Jordon, Eleanor Harz, and Mari Noda. *Japanese: The Spoken Language.* Part 1. New Haven: Yale University Press, 1987.

Kitamura, Fumio, and Yurio Ishizu. *Garden Plants in Japan.* Tokyo: Kokusai Bunka Shinkokai, 1963.

Kuck, Loraine. *The World of the Japanese Garden: From Chinese Origins to Modern Landscape Art*. New York: Weatherhill, 1980.

McFadden, Dorothy L. *Oriental Gardens in America: A Visitor's Guide*. Los Angeles: Douglas-West, 1976.

McKiernan, Kathleen. "Volunteer Guides' Handbook." Portland: Japanese Garden Society of Oregon, 1992.

Nitschke, Günter. *Japanese Gardens: Right Angles and Natural Form*. Cologne: Benedikt Taschen, 1993.

Okakura, Kakuzo. *The Book of Tea*. Edited by Everett F. Bleiler. New York: Dover Publications, 1964.

Oster, Maggie. *Reflections of the Spirit: Japanese Gardens in America*. New York: Dutton Studio Books, 1993.

Robinson, William. "Lanterns in the Garden." Unpublished typescript. Portland: Japanese Garden Society of Oregon, 1994.

———. "Silver Anniversary: History Book of the Japanese Garden Society of Oregon." Unpublished typescript. Portland: Japanese Garden Society of Oregon, 1988.

———. and Jerry White. "Plant Material in the Japanese Garden." Portland: Japanese Garden Society of Oregon, 1991.

Seike, Kiyoushi and Masanobu Kudo. *A Japanese Touch for Your Garden*. Tokyo: Kodansha International, 1992.

Tono, Takuma. *A Secret of Japanese Gardens*. N.P.: Mitsuo Onizuka, N.D.

AUTHOR'S NOTE

O ne of the author's more resilient childhood memories is of the old Portland zoo. It was a squalid place, with ugly, constricting cages that constituted inhumane and antiquated zoo design. There was a concentration camp air about the place, with its depressing small wire enclosures. Nothing about it was edifying.

In the spring of 1994, Kathy Lannigan sat next to Dorothea Lensch at a Portland State University reading by the famed Russian poet, Yevgeny Yevtushenko. They came to discuss Ms. Lensch's involvement with the publication committee at the Japanese Garden, located at the old zoo site in Portland's West Hills. Ms. Lensch felt that the committee needed some guidance. At Ms. Lannigan's suggestion the author was invited to the next committee meeting.

The author then met with the executive director of the Society, Maureen Yandle Sanchez, to propose a formal offer to write, design and produce a history of the Japanese Garden.

What you hold in your hands is the culmination of the efforts of this author and hundreds of persons who helped him produce this work.

A word of caution. It is a well-baited trap to think that one understands another culture. Equally so, it is dangerous to believe

The brilliant autumnal foliage of an Acer palmatum maple in the Natural Garden.

(Allan Mandell photograph)

that the concepts that underlie and drive and surround something as powerful as a Japanese garden are capable of facile translation into another culture. Even more dangerous is the self-delusion that someone raised outside of that culture will be able to confidently explain the underlying concepts that make up something as unique as the garden tradition of Japan.

From the onset of this project, the author has carefully tried to avoid that trap. Raised in the United States, even with a bachelor's degree in Far Eastern Studies, the author knows that he will never be able to assimilate what someone born and raised in Japan will know. Even there, in Japan, persons raised with the concepts that govern that modern country may have difficulty understanding what initiated the gardening styles of Japan, especially with gardens that are hundreds of years old.

The author remembers the story about Elaine Steinbeck, the wife of American author John Steinbeck, finding in a Yokohama bookstore a translation of *Grapes of Wrath*, which the Japanese publisher had entitled "Angry Raisins." While a humorous story, it indicates how difficult it is to translate the language and the concepts of one strong culture to another—either way.

To stay away from producing an "Angry Raisins" text, the author has used the terminology that others have used to describe many of the attributes of a Japanese garden and specifically Portland's. However, much of the language about the Garden is the author's alone; the author has tried to represent a Western, an American, an Oregonian's response to this particular place with his reactions and interpretations. The success or failure of that endeavor resides with him.

As powerful as this Garden can be—a significant transplant from a significant tradition—its placement amidst a city and region with their own definitional skews changes it. The oddity of the Portland Japanese Garden is that it is not really Japanese, though it may be more Japanese than many gardens in Japan. There is a reverence for this Garden that may be more in the tradition of gardens in Japan, without the extraordinarily heavy use that the gardens in today's Japan face, and without the modern youthful bias among young Japanese against their cultural tradition—as all modern young persons rebel against their particular culture's past.

Much of the constellating Japanese cultural baggage that is associated with the gardens (the master craftsmanship of traditional carpenters, potters, carvers, and weavers) is dying in Japan, along with the growing disinterest in the tea ceremony and *Ikebana*, for example. Without all the cultural overtones that are part of modern societal dysfunction in all current societies, a Japanese garden in America can rest in an unchallenged calmness.

This project allowed the author to revisit the site of the old Portland zoo. Each of his hundreds of forays into the wonderful ambiance of the Garden gave him renewed hope that unfortunate circumstances can be replaced by beauty and serenity. Persons with a dream and foresight—an idea that a Japanese garden would be a gift to the City of Portland and to all who enter its gates—have created a place of peace and contemplation, of renewal, of filling and emptying. It is a place that edifies.

Bruce Taylor Hamilton
Portland, Oregon

ACKNOWLEDGMENTS

GENERAL ACKNOWLEDGMENTS

Primary acknowledgment must go to Professor Takuma Tono, whose vision, patience and genius have all been proven true—and lasting—in Portland's Japanese Garden. His imprint, his concepts, remain the foundation for the look of the Portland Garden. His influence is still felt by those who knew him and worked with him. His eye still gazes on his greatest gardening creation.

To Dorothea Lensch and Kathy Lannigan who were kind enough to link the idea of the Japanese Garden book to my writing and publishing experience. Mrs. Samuel S. Johnson (and her associate Mary Krenowicz) generously provided a forested sanctuary so that the author could start writing this book. Mr. Marcus Robbins, Portland city archivist, opened numerous and varied files. Margueritte Drake, Tim Boyle, Guy Devlin, Michael Giusti, Hoichi Kurisu, Masayuki Mizuno, Rowena Newton, William Robinson, Maureen Yandle Sanchez, Mildred Schnitzer, Kathleen Serrell, Steve White, all took time to be interviewed, and add to the information in this book.

Acknowledgment must be made to those gardeners who followed Professor Tono's design, and cared for the Garden for more than a quarter of a century: Kinya Hira, Hoichi Kurisu, Hachiro Sakakibara, Michio Wakui, Masayuki Mizuno, Kichiro Sano, Takao Donuma, and Tohru Tanaka.

Snow-covered
Olympic Lantern
stands next to the inner
path of the
Flat Garden.

(Allan Mandell photograph)

The current staff of the Garden have been supportive, understanding and accepting of an interloper. Each of them in their individual way has made this project complete and lively. Each carries knowledge and experience and observational skills that enlightened and informed the author.

Head Gardener Michael Giusti—with humor and a score of years' experience—informed this text with his knowledge. Giusti's fellow gardeners (Joe Abbott, Michael Kondo, Sam Phommadouang, Fred and Jerry White) have patiently transcended the authorial eyes watching and learning while they have pursued their quiet, tending work.

The Entry Gate staff—Guy Devlin, Geoffery Dunham, and Steve White—have daily let the author enter the place that they guard, patrol and care for so passionately.

Administrative staff Darlene Dunham (gift store manager), Beth Yandle (executive secretary) and Cheryl Ching (assistant to the director) cordially allowed the author to intrude into their office space while they displayed the superb professionalism that is the hallmark of the Japanese Garden.

John Tomlinson, a long associate of the author, generously provided his remarkable talents to produce the map of the Garden used in this volume. Copy editor Sharon Elaine Thompson's eagle eye and keen mind has improved the text in so many ways.

William Robinson needs an additional nod. The author could not have done this work without all the years "Robbie" Robinson kept records. His informal history of the Garden, his recently completed typescript compilation on the Garden's lanterns, and his encyclopedic knowledge saved the author months of research time. "Ask Robbie," was the regular response to questions about the Garden's history. Phyllis Reynolds, a botanical expert, corrected many plant-name errors for the second printing.

The author reserves a special appreciation for Maureen Yandle Sanchez, the Garden's executive director. Her leadership, clear vision, and drive initiated this project. The author found unanimous high regard for Ms. Sanchez's exceptional intelligence, humor and grace. She took on this project as her own, learning the book-building business with lightning speed.

The author is only the most recent person deeply involved with Portland's Japanese Garden. It would be a foul oversight to not acknowledge the hundreds of dedicated city employees, volunteers, staff members, the Board, along with the superb support from many in Japan, and all the Japanese Garden Society members who have made this their Garden. Their work, the "human" part of nature, made the author's task easier, and provided the place of substance as the subject of this book.

All the persons noted above do not remove the author from the final and sole responsibility for the text and its contents. Any enlightened insights come from the many talented persons who have dedicated themselves to the Garden and to this project. Any errors are the author's.

PHOTOGRAPHIC ACKNOWLEDGMENTS

The author is deeply indebted to nearly a score of dedicated and talented photographers. These image makers, who have quietly entered the Garden for many years, have produced a collection of photographs without which this book would have sputtered to a stop.

With prescience and diligence, often hustling up the hill to take early morning shots when the weather is just right—many making the first tracks through the snow after an overnight fall—these remarkable men and women bring varied eyes and differing backgrounds to this publication.

Maureen Yandle Sanchez scoured her records for known photographic Garden habitués. Her energy brought to the project well over two thousand slides, transparencies and prints for scrutiny. This pile of remarkable images soon narrowed to nearly five hundred, then slimmed to two-hundred and sixty, and finally (agonizingly) dropped to the nearly one-hundred-and-fifty in this book. It was a delightful task, one that allowed the author the pleasure of entering the visual minds of some remarkable persons.

Thanks to:

Ray Atkeson (American Landscapes), Ron Cronin, C. Bruce Forster, Lawrence Hudetz, Janet Loughrey, Bruce Lellman, Allan Mandell, Duncan Neilson, Deon Reynolds, William Robinson, Rick Schafer (American Landscapes), Jerry Stelmack, Steve Terrill, David Whetstone, Allan Bruce Zee and all the other photographers who generously submitted their work for review.

ABOUT THE AUTHOR

B ruce Taylor Hamilton is an Oregon-born free-lance author, book designer and publications consultant. He has been in the business of producing fine publications for over a quarter-century, as an editor, designer and publisher.

He left Portland to pursue his university education, receiving degrees from both the University of Washington and California at Berkeley. After serving as an editor with the Mark Twain Project at the University of California for eight years, he returned to Portland and served with distinction as the director of the Oregon Historical Society Press, a position he held for seventeen years.

Hamilton has a background in letterpress printing and an advanced degree specializing in the history of printing and publishing. He has been the judge and commentator for two national university press publications competitions, and has himself designed numerous award-winning publications for both the Oregon Historical Society Press and for other publishers.

He has taught publishing courses at a number of universities, and has worked as a publications consultant with many organizations throughout the state.

A heavy, wet snow covers the Strolling Pond stream.
Trees and shrubs take on softened shape, as do the
Harp Tuner Lantern and the Moon Bridge.

(David Whetstone photograph)

THE JAPANESE GARDEN

ANTIQUE GATE	A
GARDEN HOUSE	B
ENTRY GATE	C
WISTERIA ARBOR	D
SAPPORO PAGODA LANTERN	E
LOWER POND	F
MOON BRIDGE	G
UPPER POND	H
OLD MACHIAI	I
TEA HOUSE	J
NEW MACHIAI	K
"SAKA'S POND"	L
AZUMAYA	M
PAVILION	N
GIFT SHOP	O

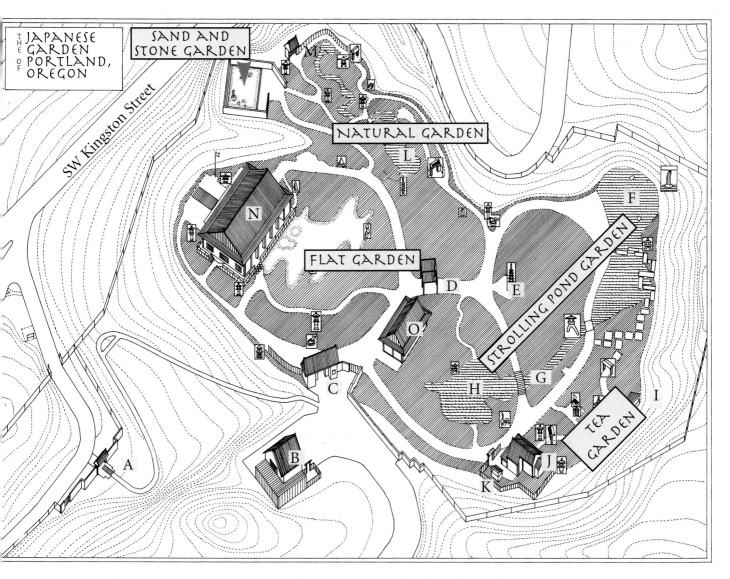

Bird's-eye view of the Japanese Garden from the northwest.

(John Tomlinson map)

147

ABOUT THE TYPEFACES

Minon, a geralde face was used for the text setting. It was designed in 1990 for the computer typeface company, Adobe, by one of that firm's most prolific designers, Robert Slimbach. It is a classical face, and old-style, remarkable for its readability. As a face designed for digital technology, it translates well from the computer's memory to the printed page.

Captions are set in ITC Flora, a san serif face designed for a German company by Gerard Unger in 1985, and named for the designer's daughter. The International Typeface Corporation issued Flora in 1989. Its design combines san serif simplicity with the basic structure of a Italian chancery hand (the later the source for the original italic used as early as 1501).

Adrian Frutiger, one of the great modern type designers, created Herculanum (a glyphic face) in 1990. It is used as the display face in this volume. (Frutiger is most famous for the san serif named for him.) Herculanum is an impressive and individual type based on first-century Roman letter forms, a cursive hand written with a stylus in clay. Herculanum was Pompeii's sister.

COLOPHON

DESIGN &
PRODUCTION

This volume was designed by Bruce Taylor Hamilton, who also
supervised its production.

EDITING

The editing of the final text was performed by Sharon Elaine
Thompson.

CARTOGRAPHY

The map of the Japanese Gardens was strikingly designed by John
Tomlinson.

COLOR SEPARATIONS
& FILM OUTPUTTING

The film of the text and the color separations were produced by
Wy'east Color of Portland, Oregon.

PRINTING & BINDING

Printing and binding were produced by Kyodo Printing, Singapore.

A view down into the Japanese Garden from a Washington Park trail.

(Lawrence Hudetz photograph)